HOW BEAUTIFUL THE WORLD COULD BE

HOW BEAUTIFUL
THE WORLD COULD BE

Christian Reflections on the Everyday

Frederick Christian Bauerschmidt

WILLIAM B. EERDMANS PUBLISHING COMPANY
GRAND RAPIDS, MICHIGAN

Wm. B. Eerdmans Publishing Co.
4035 Park East Court SE, Grand Rapids, Michigan 49546
www.eerdmans.com

© 2022 Frederick Christian Bauerschmidt
Published 2022
Printed in the United States of America

28 27 26 25 24 23 22   1 2 3 4 5 6 7

ISBN 978-0-8028-8021-5

Library of Congress Cataloging-in-Publication Data

Names: Bauerschmidt, Frederick Christian, author.
Title: How beautiful the world could be : Christian reflections
    on the everyday / Frederick Christian Bauerschmidt.
Description: Grand Rapids, Michigan : Wm. B. Eerdmans Pub-
    lishing Co., 2022. | Includes index. | Summary: "A collection
    of meditations on Christian life that locate noteworthy cur-
    rent events, cultural trends, and particular occasions within
    the larger story of Scripture"—Provided by publisher.
Identifiers: LCCN 2021031625 | ISBN 9780802880215
Subjects: LCSH: Christianity and culture--Sermons. | Chris-
    tian life—Sermons. | Bauerschmidt, Frederick Christian—
    Sermons. | Catholic Church—Sermons. | BISAC:
    RELIGION / Christianity / General | RELIGION /
    Christian Living / Spiritual Growth
Classification: LCC BR115.C8 B3855 2022 | DDC 261—dc23
LC record available at https://lccn.loc.gov/2021031625

*To the people of Corpus Christi Catholic Church
in Baltimore, Maryland*

Contents

Introduction

We human beings are creatures of everydayness. We have no choice but to find ourselves at a particular place in a particular moment. When we seek to speak of the eternal God in our particular place and moment, it is inevitably a word in time that we speak, a human word that seeks to reflect the beauty of God's timeless Word, a word that is likewise heard in time by listeners who share with us that place and moment, that particular slice of the everyday. And those slices of the everyday are fleeting; sounding forth in that particular moment, our words accompany that moment in its decay into the remembered—and often *mis*remembered—past.

The great mystery of the incarnation is that the timeless Word took on creaturely everydayness, giving us hope that our own time*ful* words might not entirely miss their mark when we come to speak of eternal mysteries. But even the most on-target theological utterance is still subject to time's decay. As someone who has spent over a quarter century studying and teaching the works of theologians from the past, I have some sense of how time-bound all of theology is, and of the immense labor involved in trying to release theological words from the bonds of time, and of the ultimate futility of any hope to fully liberate theology from its now-lost moment. If one keeps peeling back the onion of historical particularity, there is eventually nothing left. Our theological language, no less than our "ordinary" language, speaks from and to the particular. It is thoroughly embedded in our everyday life.

Preaching is theology at perhaps its most particular. As I began thinking of assembling a collection of homilies, I went back through about a dozen years' worth of homilies. I found myself drawn to those that spoke to specific occasions and people rather than those that might be of more general interest. As I reflected on what I valued in these homilies, it occurred to me that it was precisely their ephemeral everydayness that gave them life. They, like their author and their audience, were creatures of time and space, and so were more suited to our creaturely condition than words that aspired to some sort of false timeless universality.

I often say that the worst sermons are those that could have been preached at any time and in any place to any group of listeners. I sometimes refer to them as "sermons downloaded from the internet," not because I actually think that they have been plagiarized (though on occasion I have wondered), but because they might as well have been. What they lack is everydayness. They not only show no awareness of the congregations in which they are being preached, but they also show no awareness of what might be taking place in the wider world or church or even, apart from being tied to the correct lectionary cycle, what year it is. I suppose such sermons have the advantage of being recyclable, but that seems a small advantage.

This does not, of course, mean that preaching should be utterly opaque outside its immediate context. We should seek not only to pull the Scriptures into our moment but to pull our moment into the Scriptures, and it is because of this that those moments can be something more than of merely passing interest. Some of the events that occasioned homilies in this book remain seared in our collective consciousness; others have faded from memory. What makes them of lasting interest, however, is not how well they have retained their cultural purchase, but how they have illuminated the presence of the Word in the world. In a sense, when we preach to the particularities of life, we place them within the frame of eternity. And in doing so, we seek to show how beautiful the world might be, even in its darkest moments, when the light of the gospel shines upon it.

I have arranged the homilies that follow into six sections, each with its own brief introduction. Five of the sections represent different kinds of everydayness: the everyday of current events in the world, the everyday of cultural phenomena, the everyday of events in the wider church, the everyday of the feasts of the liturgical year, and the everyday of key moments in the lives of individuals and communities. A sixth section includes homilies given during the early months of the coronavirus pandemic, which I suppose became for many of us its own sort of everyday. The homilies within each section are arranged in chronological order, and each homily has its own context-setting introduction, both to provide information that might make sense of specific references, as well as to offer a bit of metacommentary reflecting on what I thought I was doing in the homily.

Because these were originally written for oral delivery, they were composed using sense lines to aid in that delivery. By retaining the sense lines here, I hope to preserve a bit of the oral context for which these homilies were crafted, as yet another way of acknowledging their particularity. I also believe that this format can aid in a meditative reading of them, forcing readers to pace their reading in something like the way that the preacher paces his or her oral delivery.

With the exception of the Corona Time homilies and a handful of others, these homilies were preached at Corpus

Christi Catholic Church in Baltimore, Maryland, which is my family's parish and where I was assigned as a deacon from 2007 to 2019. This is a small urban parish that draws its congregation from all over the Baltimore area and is firmly committed to fostering the full, conscious, and active participation of the laity in the worship of the church. As such, the parishioners are not afraid to tell a preacher what they think about what they have heard, and they have taught me much through their honesty and patience. They have also always demanded preaching that spoke to the moments, fleeting though they may be, of our collective life together. I dedicate this book to them.

PART I

News Cycles

The great Swiss Protestant theologian Karl Barth is famous for saying that preachers should preach with the Bible in one hand and the newspaper in the other. Of course, like many things people are famous for saying, that's not exactly what he said. Late in life, he was quoted in *Time* magazine saying that his advice for young theologians had always been, "take your Bible and take your newspaper, and read both. But interpret newspapers from your Bible" (*Time*, May 31, 1963). This statement not only fits with Barth's theology, which begins from God's revealed word, but also offers sound advice for preachers in dealing with current events.

Things happen in the world and preachers must respond to them, to cast the light of the gospel upon them. But this is a risky business. The risks are several:

- You can succumb to the insta-pundit temptation, feeling compelled by events to say something before you've had time to adequately reflect on either the gospel or the events.
- You can let events set the agenda, ignoring the appointed readings or twisting them to address events that they don't really address.

- You can polarize your congregation with preaching that is overly partisan, or at least appears to some to be so.
- You can preach on a very narrow set of current issues (such as abortion, religious freedom, poverty, or the death penalty) and annoy those who do not share your hobbyhorses while making those who do share them feel smug and self-satisfied. The message of the gospel is broad enough that it should make everyone uncomfortable at some point.
- You can betray the gospel by preaching about events in the world in a way that is so bland that no one could ever possibly be offended.

The risks, however, are worth running because Christians live in the world and what is in the news is often what is on their minds, and the preacher has an obligation to try to locate the ongoing story of the world within the Christian story. Some may be angered by what you say, thinking you are bringing politics into the pulpit. And being politically partisan and divisive is a real risk. When preaching on divisive topics you must always:

- make sure that you have tried as hard as you can to understand what is being said on both sides of the issue,
- make sure that you have interpreted what is being said by those you disagree with as charitably as reason and reality will allow, and
- make sure that what you say is solidly in accord with the basic teachings of the wider church.

Of course, even if you do this, you may still end up exacerbating divisions. But if the Christian story is kept front and center, many will be willing to grapple with trying to see events from the standpoint of the gospel.

This is at least what I have tried to do with the homilies collected in this section, all of which relate in one way or another to events current in the news cycle when they were preached. I cannot claim that I always grasped the true significance of the events—part of what it means to live in time is that you often have to go back and rethink what you thought you knew—but all of these were attempts to interpret the newspaper (or whatever form of media) through the Bible.

1. The Fear Gauge

The financial collapse of 2008 is, in retrospect, one of the key events
of the early twenty-first century, revealing the rapacity that drives
much of the world's economy and in many ways reigniting an
interest in what are typically called "progressive" politics, espe-
cially among young people. At the time, however, there was simply
a sense of panic as financial institutions failed, mortgages were
foreclosed, and retirement funds lost value. For me, having been
ordained in the spring of 2007, this homily felt like the first time
that I was able to move out of theological lecture mode and ad-
dress what was happening in the lives of my listeners.

READINGS: Isaiah 25:6–10a; Psalm 23;
   Philippians 4:12–14, 19–20; Matthew 22:1–10

On Friday, the good news
was that the trading day on Wall Street closed
with the Dow Jones Industrial Average
down only 128 points.
The bad news
was that this ended a week
in which the Dow lost 1,874 points,
over twenty percent of its value.

This week Russia, Indonesia, and Ukraine
suspended trading on their stock exchanges
to try to prevent the instability of US financial markets
from infecting their economies,
and the country of Iceland
teetered on the verge of bankruptcy.
And in what is certainly
the most ominous-sounding bit of news,
the Chicago Board Options Exchange Volatility Index,
known as the "fear gauge,"

climbed to its fifth-consecutive record level.
I must admit that such news
makes my own "Volatility Index,"
my own personal "fear gauge," begin to rise,
not least because I'm not exactly sure
that I completely understand the financial news
with which I'm being bombarded,
nor do I really feel that I am in a position
to even begin to evaluate the proffered solutions:
Should the government intervene?
And if so, is the right amount of money
being spent on the right things?
I just know that, this past week,
when I made the mistake
of opening the quarterly report
from my TIAA-CREF retirement fund
it seemed that I had somehow lost a lot of money
without ever having the pleasure of spending it
and I could feel my volatility index—my fear gauge—
rising to record heights.

Why regale you with news of the business world
and of my own personal anxiety?
Because I suspect that many of you

have also looked at your retirement plans
or stock portfolios this week,
or at least been subjected to the ever-rising tone
of anxiety about the economy in the news media.
Some might even have more immediate worries
of losing a job or a home.
And I suspect your fear gauge is also rising.

What consolation can the word of God offer us today?
Our Gospel reading for today seems to depict a situation
in which the volatility index is off the charts,
with invited banquet guests
killing those who bring them their invitations
(wouldn't a simple "no thank you" have sufficed?)
and the king who is throwing the banquet retaliating,
not just by killing the invited guests,
but by destroying their entire city.
You just want to say, "OK, everybody take a deep breath."
But our other readings sound a quite different note,
a note of confidence,
a note of faith that we will be able
to weather the storms of life,
a note of hope that our fear gauge
does not have to grow inexorably higher.

In our second reading,
from Paul's letter to the Philippians,
Paul tells us that he has learned the secret
of living in abundance and of being in need,
of being well fed and of going hungry.

Of course, the ups and downs of Paul's fortune
do not have to do
with the ups and downs of the stock market

but with the fact that he writes from a Roman prison
and does not know if he will ever see freedom again.
Still, as different as Paul's problems may be from ours,
we might be interested in knowing
what the secret of his equanimity is,
what the secret is
that keeps his fear gauge
in the lower numbers
despite the rather dire situation
in which he finds himself.

8

His secret is not, as we might first suspect,
that he has simply detached himself from life,
so that he does not care and has no opinion
about how he would like things to turn out.
Paul would have been quite familiar
with such a strategy,
since it was the one taught
by the Stoic philosophers of his day:
One preserves oneself from life's fortunes
by not clinging and not caring.
But it is not this path of stoic indifference that he takes;
rather, his secret, which he quite openly shares, is this:
"I can do all things in him that strengthens me."
Paul's secret for controlling his fear gauge
is not to keep himself from caring,
not to keep himself from clinging,
but to care passionately about
and cling tightly to
the one who, as he puts it,
"will fully supply whatever you need."
Paul believes, with Isaiah in our first reading,
that "the Lord God will wipe away

the tears from every face."
Paul believes, with our psalmist,
that "the Lord *is* my shepherd"
and "I *shall* not want."

But notice that this hope
about which Paul cares passionately
and to which he clings tightly
does not promise that Paul will not be in need
or that he will not be hungry;
it does not promise that he
will ever be released from prison.
Paul's secret is his faith that in Christ he has a hope
that can never be defeated by life's circumstances,
because, in Christ, God has come
to share our circumstances,
so that in all our circumstances—
whether imprisonment or financial loss
or any other situation that sets our fear gauge rising—
we can find the presence of God that will sustain us.
If we can fix our eyes on what Paul calls
God's "glorious riches in Christ Jesus,"
if we see the circumstances of our lives
as pervaded by God's sustaining presence,
then we can find hope and we can conquer fear,
no matter what storms batter us.

This, of course, is easier said than done;
it requires that we cultivate a capacity
to pay attention to God's presence in our lives,
a capacity that is planted in us by God's grace,
that grows through prayer,
that is nourished through the sacraments.

But perhaps we might start
by simply attending
to our own personal volatility indexes,
and when we feel our fear gauge rising,
to make our own prayer be the words of Paul:
"I can do all things in Christ who strengthens me."

2. Love

The event that occasioned this homily was not of the scope of a financial collapse or a national election, but was more local—local not only to the Baltimore community but also to the community of the university where I teach. A student was surprised to receive a call from her father saying that the family was in town and asking if she would come join them for dinner. When she arrived at the hotel where they were staying, her father, having already killed her mother and sister, killed her and then took his own life, apparently motivated by shame over financial losses and a pending investigation of his involvement in a Ponzi scheme. In using her story in this homily, I hope that, rather than exploiting this horror, I was genuinely struggling with the meaning of love and the distortions to which love might fall prey.

READINGS: Acts 10:25–26, 34–35, 44–48; 1 John 4:7–10; John 15:9–17

Saint Thomas Aquinas,
at the end of his lengthy commentary on John's Gospel,
recounts the medieval legend that "as an old man
John was carried to the church by his followers
to teach the faithful.

He taught only one thing:
'Little children, love one another.'"
Then Thomas adds,
"This is the perfection
of the Christian life" (*Commentary on John* n. 2653).

This is a legend and not from Scripture,
but it rings true
with our second reading and Gospel for today,
both of which are traditionally ascribed to Saint John
and both of which place love
at the center of their message.
From the First Letter of John:
"Let us love one another,
because love is of God."
From our Gospel:
"This I command you: love one another."
This is the perfection of the Christian life:
to know the one, true and living God.
We come to know God by loving because God is love,
and when we love,
we know God from the inside, as it were.

This sounds like pretty good news.
Love: this is the commandment of Christ to his disciples.
Disciples who love will "bear fruit that will remain."
What could be more simple than that?
As Saint Augustine said,
"Love, and do what you will" (*Homilies on 1 John* 7.8).

But anyone who loves knows
that love is really not simple at all.
Our feelings about people and things

can be complex and conflicted.
Our love finds itself entangled
with a host of emotions and passions,
not excluding anger, jealousy, lust and pride,
which makes it difficult for us to separate what is love
from what might be something else,
some darker impulse,
that has attached itself to our love,
or that masquerades as love.
People bind themselves to others in the name of love,
but they also break those bonds in the name of love.
People die in the name of love,
but they also kill in the name of love.
Saint Augustine's injunction,
"love, and do what you will,"
can be twisted so that any action on our part
can be justified
so long as we do it in the name of love.

This has been on my mind recently
particularly in light of the highly publicized murder
of a student at Loyola College, where I teach.
She, along with her mother and sister,
was killed by her father,
who then took his own life.
I did not know this student personally,
but the impact of her murder on her friends,
many of whom are my students,
and the particular nature of this crime,
a father murdering his family,
has caused me to reflect on this event
more than I might on the typical human tragedy
that confronts me in my morning paper.

I don't think anyone yet knows what role, if any,
mental illness might have played in this tragedy,
and how this might affect
our understanding of her father's actions.
But what has haunted me
is that this man who killed his wife and children
appears from all reports to have loved them.
What haunts me more is that he quite possibly thought
that he was taking their lives *because* he loved them—
that he was somehow protecting them,
or ensuring that he could have them with him
even in death.
Could it be that he used love
as the justification for his actions?

"Love, and do what you will"?
In this case, surely not.
This man may have loved his family.
That is not my place to judge.
But this was *not* an act that was born out of love,
but out of some darker passion
that hid behind the mask of love.
Surely there are actions
that are simply incompatible with love,
and yet our human love can become so twisted by sin
that we attempt to justify these actions
in the name of love.
This is an extreme example,
but the shadow of sin falls across us all
and if I am honest with myself
I find that my love, too,
is not immune from the darker impulses
of the human species.

But thanks be to God that all this talk about love
that we hear in today's readings
is not first and foremost
about our human love at all.
Our second reading says:
"This is love:
not that we have loved God,
but that he loved us
and sent his Son
as expiation for our sins."
This phrase, "expiation for our sins,"

is perhaps somewhat ominous
and technical sounding,
but what it means
is that God has sent us Jesus
to redeem the failures of our love.
We are to love one another
not according to the pattern
of our fallen human love—
a love that has become entwined
with other, darker passions—
but with the pure love
that Christ showed on the cross,
the love that lays down its life
so as to give new life.
This is the pattern of true love
in which we are to abide,
and the good news of Jesus Christ
is that God gives it to us as a gift
because God is love.
It is not something that we achieve,
but something that God achieves in us.
Through the free gift of God's love

our human love can,
over the course of a lifetime,
begin to be untwisted,
disentangled from those dark passions
that hide within it.
It can be remade
according to the pattern of Christ's love.
In the waters of baptism love can be purified
because we are immersed in God's own love.
At the table of the Eucharist,
true love can be nourished in us,
because the love of God
becomes our food and drink.
This is the gift of love in which we are to abide.
This is the love that Christ commands.
This is the perfection of the Christian life.

3. Who Sinned?

News cycles provide, with depressing regularity, opportunities to **17**
grapple with the problem of evil—both the moral evil of cruel and
corrupt human behavior and the "natural evil" of various disas-
ters. The Haitian earthquake, which killed a quarter of a million
people, was more than a year in the past when I preached this
homily, and the tsunami that killed twenty thousand people in
Japan had occurred the month before, but questions about belief
in God's goodness in the face of evil seem to be perennial. In this
homily I did not try to answer those questions, not least because
I am not sure they are answerable, but rather I pointed to the hope
held out to us in the Gospel.

READINGS: 1 Samuel 16:1b, 6–7, 10–13a;
Ephesians 5:8–14; John 9

Confronted with a man who was born blind,
Jesus's disciples ask,
"Who sinned, this man or his parents?"
A devastating earthquake hits the island of Haiti,
and American televangelist (and sometime politician)
Pat Robertson asks whether this might be
because of a pact

the Haitians had made centuries ago with the devil.
Who sinned, the Haitians or their parents?
An even stronger earthquake
and the resultant tsunami
pushes Japan to the brink of a nuclear crisis,
and the governor of Tokyo asks
whether this might not be divine punishment.
Who sinned, the Japanese or their parents?

We might think that, faced with such misery,
we would never raise such insensitive questions,
but it is a natural human response to misfortune
to ask why such things happen,
to ask who is to blame,
to seek some past action on someone's part
that would justify the pain and suffering
that has occurred.
We desire to find order in the world,
for if we can figure out
how misfortune and disaster
are connected to someone's past action
then the perplexity that accompanies such events
might be dissipated
and we can restore our belief
that the world really is, despite all appearances,
a reasonable, just, and orderly place.

But Jesus approaches the misery and misfortune
of the man born blind
in a different way:
In response to his disciples' question
he says, "Neither he nor his parents sinned;
it is so that the works of God

might be made visible through him."
Jesus then spits on the ground,
makes a muddy paste,
and, rubbing it in the man's eyes,
heals him and restores his sight.

I don't think Jesus is saying
that God blinded this man from birth
just so that Jesus could come along,
decades later,
and heal him.

Rather, he is indicating to his disciples that,
when confronted with human suffering,
they are asking the wrong sort of question.
They are seeking an explanation
of where misfortune comes from:
Why was this man born blind?
Why must the suffering
of the poverty-stricken people of Haiti
be magnified by a terrible earthquake?
What did the people of Japan do
to deserve a catastrophic tsunami?
But these sorts of questions are unanswerable,
or at least whatever answers God has to them
are probably not the kind of thing
we mere mortals might understand.
Instead, Jesus redirects the attention of his disciples
from the question of the reason for suffering
to the ministry of alleviating suffering.
The source of the misery and misfortune
of the man born blind
remains hidden.
What is visible is

the healing,
saving,
enlightening
power of Jesus.
What is visible is the ministry of Jesus,
the light of the world.
Into the darkness of the man born blind
Jesus brings his light,
both to heal the man's physical blindness
and to give to him the eyes of faith
so that he might recognize the power of God
in the one who has healed him.

Having been enlightened by Jesus,
the man becomes himself a source of light,
bearing witness to Jesus
before those who would oppose him.
This remarkable transformation
from darkness to light
is echoed in our second reading,
from Paul's letter to the Ephesians:
"Brothers and sisters:
You were once darkness,
but now you are light in the Lord."
Notice that Paul says to the Ephesians
not simply that they have *received*
light in their darkness,
but that they have *become* light.
The light that they have received
they are now to share with others.
In other words,
now that they have received Christ's light
they are called to share in Jesus's ministry

of healing,
saving,
and enlightening.
Notice that in today's Gospel
Jesus says to his disciples,
"We have to do the works
of the one who sent me
while it is day."
Not *I*, but *we*.
The disciples are called to share
in Jesus's ministry of light in darkness.

Faced with human misery and misfortune,
whether that of the man born blind
or the disasters of our own day,
true followers of Christ must not let
the inevitable questions about "why"
distract them from answering Jesus's call
to join in his ministry of light:
"Awake, O sleeper,
and arise from the dead,
and Christ will give you light."
Through the light of Christ,
we become light.
And, transformed into light,
we can respond to the call
that he gave to the disciples
who witnessed his transfigured glory:
"Rise, and do not be afraid."
Rise, and join him in being light
in the darkest places
of human misery and misfortune.

4. Uprising

22   *Baltimore, where I have lived for over a quarter century, is known*
nationally as a place plagued by crime and violence, an image
emblazoned in people's minds by the death in police custody
of a young Black man, Freddie Gray, and the civil unrest that
followed. But the reality of Baltimore is more complex. Part of
that complex reality is that well-off people like me can find it an
extremely congenial place to live, in large part because we live
insulated from the reality of the daily violence that shapes and
shatters the lives of our fellow citizens like Freddie Gray. But the
event of his death and its aftermath drove home that reality in a
way that could not be ignored.

READINGS: Acts 10:25–26, 34–35, 44–48; 1 John 4:7–10;
John 15:9–17

Though we have moved, thank God,
out of the top story slot
on the cable news programs,
with their endlessly repeated video loops
of the burning CVS at Penn and North,
our city continues to struggle to understand
the events of the past few weeks.

Part of this is the struggle of how to describe
what happened on April 27,
a week ago this past Monday.
Was it looting?
A riot?
An uprising?
I suspect that it was in some measure
all three of these at once.
But most of all it was a sign, a symptom
of an underlying disease in our society—
a disease of violence and injustice,
of racism and despair,
a disease that manifests itself
in the poorest parts of our city
but for which we all bear responsibility.

If a sacrament is,
as Saint Augustine said,
an outward and visible sign
of an inward and invisible grace,
then the violence of April 27
was something like an anti-sacrament:
an outward and visible sign
of a pervasive violence and injustice
that is invisible to many of us
but which too many
of our brothers and sisters in this city
live with on a daily basis.
It was not simply a sign of the personal moral failures
of those who damaged property or looted businesses,
but of our collective moral failure as a society
to make good on our talk of justice and equality.
I think that for many of us these past few weeks

have been a time of soul-searching,
a time in which we have been forced by events
to ask ourselves
how we could have ignored for so long
the truths about our city
now made manifest to us.
We have been forced by events
to ask ourselves
what we can do
and from where we can draw our hope
as we seek a city that is more peaceful
because it is more just.

The Austrian psychiatrist Viktor Frankl
recounts a story from his experience
in a Nazi death camp:
"One evening,
when we were already resting
on the floor of our hut,
dead tired, soup bowls in hand,
a fellow prisoner rushed in
and asked us to run out to the assembly grounds
and see the wonderful sunset.
Standing outside we saw sinister clouds
glowing in the west
and the whole sky alive with clouds
of ever-changing shapes and colors,
from steel blue to blood red.
The desolate grey mud huts
provided a sharp contrast,
while the puddles on the muddy ground
reflected the glowing sky.
Then, after minutes of moving silence,

one prisoner said to another,
'How beautiful the world *could* be!'"

It seems to me that when we gather
to celebrate the sacraments
it is like the beauty of the sunset
reflecting in the puddles
of that desolate, gray death camp.
God's grace, at work in the sacraments,
is a thing of great beauty
shining on a world of sin and injustice.
It is the grace that, in our first reading,
welcomed the household of the gentile Cornelius
into the family of God,
the God who, as Saint Peter exclaims,
"shows no partiality."
It is the grace that takes us
from being slaves to sin
and makes us into friends of Christ
and of each other in Christ.
It is the grace of the God
whom we can only know through love,
the God who *is* love.
And when we baptize,
when we break bread,
when we anoint,
when we absolve,
that beauty shines upon us,
transforming death into life
drawing us along with Jesus
in his passing over
from the tomb of death
to the life of glory.

But while the sacraments
make real and present to us
the beauty of God's grace,
they should also make us ever more aware
of the graceless violence and hideous injustice
suffered in the hidden corners of our city,
our nation,
our world.
It shouldn't take the anti-sacrament of a riot
to make us face up to the injustice
suffered by our brothers and sisters,
not when we baptize in order to free from bondage,
not when we gather each week to remember
the legally sanctioned injustice
of the death of Jesus.
The sacraments should not simply console us
with the beauty of God's grace.
They should awaken within us
a holy impatience,
a holy sense of outrage,
an awareness of how beautiful the world *could* be
but is not—not yet—
for those confined within places of death.

Christ calls us his friends
and calls us to be friends with one another.
The God who shows no partiality
calls us to cross the barriers
of race and ethnicity, class and culture.
The past few weeks have shown us how difficult
that seemingly simple command is.
What would it mean if we took this vision
of how beautiful the world *could* be

and lived it outside these walls?
It's hard for me to imagine, honestly.
In the past few weeks
my eyes have been transfixed
by the ugliness of injustice.
But here at this altar we catch a glimpse
of the beauty that could be,
when the friendship of all God's people
will be present not in sacramental signs
but in the reality of the kingdom
of the God who is love.
May our celebration today fill us
with the grace of holy impatience
for the coming of that kingdom.

5. War on Mercy

SECOND SUNDAY OF ADVENT

DECEMBER 6, 2015

28 *As I looked through my past homilies for this collection, I found a disturbing number of them that made reference to mass shootings. I have included this one, which speaks of both the December 2, 2015, shooting in San Bernardino, California, by two people killing in the name of the Islamic State (ISIS), and of the November 27, 2015, shooting at a Planned Parenthood clinic in Colorado Springs, Colorado, by a man killing as "a warrior for the babies." As usual, politicians spoke of sending their "thoughts and prayers," though this time such sentiments met with critical backlash. I felt it was important to recognize the legitimate critique of anodyne invocations of prayer, while at the same time pressing beyond immediate events to the deeper dysfunction of the human race, a dysfunction that, indeed, only God can fix.*

READINGS: Baruch 5:1–9; Philippians 1:4–6, 8–11; Luke 3:1–6

They killed without mercy in San Bernardino.
They killed without mercy
fourteen coworkers and acquaintances,
alongside whom they had previously
lived their lives in peace.

They killed without mercy,
seemingly in the name of God,
the God whom the Qur'an invokes
at the outset of every chapter
as "the Compassionate, the Merciful."

He, too, killed without mercy in Colorado Springs.
He killed without mercy or discrimination
three people who happened to fall
within the sights of his weapon.
He killed without mercy,
seemingly in the name of God,
the God whom he was convinced
would mercifully cover his sins,
no matter what he did.

Some of us reacted
by taking to Facebook and Twitter,
posting and tweeting
our "thoughts and prayers" for the victims;
others of us rebuked these sentiments,
saying that thoughts and prayers are not enough,
that concrete action must be taken
to end such violence.
Many of us simply felt
immense perplexity and sadness.
We huddled,
wrapped in our robe
of mourning and misery—
wanting to pray
but not knowing what to say,
wanting to act
but not knowing what to do,

wanting maybe simply
to hide and hope it all would go away.

I am not without sympathy
for the New York *Daily News*,
which responded to the politicians
who sent out their "thoughts and prayers"
with a headline that read,
"God isn't fixing this."
I'm sympathetic because I too grow tired
of politicians and pundits
who turn prayer into a placeholder
for prudent action infinitely delayed.
I too sense with weary irony
the ambiguities of praying to God
for those who have been killed in the name of God
by those who probably also prayed to God
before embarking on their merciless missions.

But even my weariness and my cynicism
cannot keep me from calling out,
"Lord, have mercy."
Aware of the ambiguity and abuse
that sometimes accompanies
talk of thoughts and prayers
I still cannot suppress the primal cry
that wells up
from the depth of my heart:
"Lord Jesus, have mercy on us."
We should never be ashamed to pray
in response to the horrors of the world,
to beg that God would have mercy on this human race,
a people that has,

as Saint Catherine of Siena put it,
"declared war on [God's] mercy
and become [God's] enemies" (*Dialogue*, chapter 13).

Yes, we must act to try to curb
the merciless violence
that afflicts our nation and our world,
but we must also recognize
that this violence has roots
deep within our human nature,
a nature that has been devastated by sin.
There are things we can and should fix,
but there are also things wrong with us
that only God can fix.
The overt acts of war against God's mercy
that we witness in California or Colorado
grow from seeds of destruction
that we all have in our hearts—
seeds of resentment and pride,
seeds of spite and selfishness,
seeds of indifference and malice.
I too am at war with God's mercy;
I too am a merciless combatant
in sin's war against goodness.
Perhaps we should not expect God
to fix those situations
that call for the exercise of human wisdom
and political prudence,
but surely I must beg God to fix my warring heart.
Confronted with the darkness around and within me,
I am not ashamed to call out:
Come, God of mercy,
come and bring us back

from the darkness of our exile;
come and take from us
the robe of mourning and misery.

And so we gather together on this day
as God's people,
seeking God's mercy.
And we hear in our Gospel
the voice of John the Baptist,
"Prepare the way of the Lord,
make straight his paths. . . .
And all flesh shall see the salvation of God."
We hear the voice of the prophet Baruch:
"Take off your robe of mourning and misery;
put on the splendor of glory from God forever. . . .
For God is leading Israel in joy
by the light of his glory,
with his mercy and justice for company."
In this season of Advent,
we light our candles of hope,
visible signs of our prayer that God's mercy
would bring peace to our hearts and to our world.
We light our candles of hope
because we believe that God *has* come to us,
that in the life, death, and rising of Jesus
God *has*, as Saint Catherine of Siena wrote,
"[given] this warring human race a way to reconciliation,
bringing great peace out of our war"
(*Dialogue*, chapter 13).
Yes, we must act to restrain
the violence that grows
from our war against God's mercy.
But we must also pray for that mercy,

because in the end
it is only God's mercy
that will disarm our hearts.
In the face of merciless killings
done in the name of a merciful God,
we light our candles of hope
as a sign of our prayer
that God the Compassionate,
the Merciful,
will one day reign victorious
and that we will find ourselves
joyfully defeated,
prisoners of war
who have surrendered to mercy.

6. Speaking Your Mind

SIXTH SUNDAY IN ORDINARY TIME

FEBRUARY 12, 2017

34 *The presidential administration of Donald Trump provided so much rich homiletic material that I had to restrain myself from making him and those around him the focus each time I preached. Such restraint was important, first, because I did not want to give him the attention he so obviously craved and, second, because the congregation to which I was preaching was not filled with fans of the President. I feared I would simply have been tempting them to fall into the trap of the Pharisee's prayer, "God, I thank you that I am not like other [i.e., Republican] men." But on occasion the outrages were too egregious, or the examples too on point, to ignore, and I put restraint aside. In this instance, it was early in the Trump administration and it was easy to be somewhat light-hearted about his distinctive presidential style.*

READINGS: Sirach 15:15–20; 1 Corinthians 2:6–10; Matthew 5:17–37

Sean Spicer, the president's press secretary,
recently commented,
"Part of the reason the president got elected
is because he speaks his mind.
He doesn't hold it back,

he's authentic"
(White House press briefing, February 9, 2017).
I think we can all agree,
whatever we may think
of our president and his mind,
that no one could ever accuse him
of not speaking it.
And in our Gospel reading today
Jesus seems to commend this practice
of speaking one's mind,
telling his disciples not to swear oaths,
but to "let your 'Yes' mean 'Yes'
and your 'No' mean 'No.'"

But Jesus is not simply commending
being forthright for its own sake—
being, as they say, a "straight shooter"
(now *there's* a metaphor for you),
who lets people know what is on his or her mind.
Jesus is calling his disciples and calling us
not simply to speak our minds,
but to speak the truth.
He is telling us, his followers,
that we are not to swear oaths
but to let our "Yes" mean "Yes"
and our "No" mean "No"
because our lives ought at *all* times to testify
to the truth of the words we speak.

Hilary of Poitiers, writing in the fourth century,
said, "Those who are living
in the simplicity of faith
have no need for the ritual of an oath.

With such people, what is, always is,
and what is not, is not.
For this reason,
their every word and deed
are always truthful" (*On Matthew* 4.23).
If you need to swear an oath
in order to get people to believe what you say,
to believe not simply that *you* believe it,
but that what you believe is *true*,
then, Jesus says, something has gone wrong
in your life as his disciple.
The practice of speaking some words under oath
casts a shadow of doubt over the words
that we do not speak under oath.
It implies that we are bound to speak the truth
only at some times but not at others.
In a world pervaded
by lies and falsehoods, however,
the followers of Jesus are called
to be people of the truth at *all* times—
not simply to speak their minds,
but to have in them the mind of Christ
and to speak the truth of Christ plainly
in all their words and in all their deeds.

In our second reading Paul says that we speak
"not a wisdom of this age,
nor of the rulers of this age who are passing away.
Rather, we speak God's wisdom, mysterious, hidden,
which . . . none of the rulers of this age knew."
What is this wisdom, what is this truth,
that the powerful of the world have missed,
have overlooked,

have been blind to,
and that we are called to speak?
When Paul says that
"if they had known [this wisdom],
they would not have crucified the Lord of glory,"
he suggests that what the Jewish and Roman leaders
did not know, could not see,
is that the one whom they crucified
is the Lord of glory.
What the mighty of Jesus's day could not see,
the wisdom and truth to which they were blind,
is that the Lord of glory does not appear among us
clothed in the trappings of power,
but as one unjustly accused,
one tortured and humiliated,
one executed by the ruling imperial regime
as a threat to public order.
He appears among us as the truth crucified
by the powerful lies of our world.

This is the wisdom that Paul proclaims;
this is the truth that Jesus
calls his disciples to speak plainly;
this is the mystery hidden
from those who rule our world,
but made plain to those
who have received the Spirit of God:
The Lord of glory is not to be found
among the powerful and the wealthy,
whose power and wealth are destined to pass away,
but among the poor, those on the margins,
the outcast, the refugee, the immigrant,
the homeless one in our streets,

the child in the womb.
God chose to come among us
in the form of lowliness,
and God chooses still to be found
in those who have nothing,
in those who are defenseless and voiceless.
Jesus calls us to seek him there—
not in the halls of power,
where powerful people speak their minds
from positions of privilege,

but among the powerless.
We are to speak plainly
the truth of God's presence there,
and witness boldly to the power of the Spirit
who has revealed this hidden wisdom to us,
by giving comfort to the sick,
food to the hungry,
clothing to the naked,
refuge to the stranger.
"Whatever you did
for one of these least ones,
you did for me."

This is the truth we are called to speak.
The book of Sirach tells us
that we have before us
life and death, good and evil,
and that whichever we choose
shall be given to us.
We also have before us truth and lies—
the truth of the crucified Lord of glory
and the lies of those who killed him
in the name of public order.

Whichever we choose will be given to us.
Let us choose to speak the truth of Christ
in the face of the world's death-dealing lies;
let us choose to speak not our own minds
but the mind of Christ,
and let our "Yes" mean yes
to the God of life and compassion
and our "No" mean no
to the powers of death and fear,
which even now are passing away,
defeated by the truth
of the crucified Lord of glory.

7. Protest

40 *On September 5, 2017, President Donald Trump announced that he was ending the Deferred Action for Childhood Arrivals (DACA) program (something that he never quite fully succeeded in doing). Official protest from the bishops of the Roman Catholic Church in the US came swiftly, since the just treatment of immigrants is a core principle of Catholic social teaching (and, I would add, the gospel). Though most members of the congregation to which I was preaching were in strong agreement with the bishops on DACA, they were sometimes less than enthusiastic when they spoke on other topics. I took the occasion not only to communicate the content of the bishops' statement but also to reflect on the calling to prophetic protest against injustice, a calling that is (or at least should be) something distinct from political meddling, and one that should challenge people across the political spectrum.*

READINGS: Ezekiel 33:7–9; Romans 13:8–10;
Matthew 18:15–20

Many people
of various political persuasions
love participating in protests.
They love the exhilaration that comes

with marching in the streets
and speaking truth to power;
the deep sense of solidarity
of a people united
in standing up for what is right
and holding evil-doers accountable.

I am not one of those people.

While I have done my share of marching—
protesting wars and police brutality,
advocating for nuclear arms reduction
and a more just economic system—
I can't say that I have ever enjoyed it all that much.
I am the type of person who can't help wondering
even as I march—especially as I march—
whether all this marching is really going anywhere,
whether power listens when you speak truth to it,
whether the people united will *really* never be defeated.
I look around at the signs that others carry
and say to myself,
"I'm not sure that I entirely agree
with the precise wording of that sentiment."
I join in chanting slogans,
while at the same time thinking, "Well, you know,
the issue is really a bit more complicated than this."

And yet our Scriptures today seem to say
that when you see wrong being done,
when you see people separating themselves
from God's love by their evil actions,
you have a moral obligation to raise your voice,
to call them to repentance and conversion.

God tells the prophet Ezekiel in our first reading
that he must "speak out
to dissuade the wicked from his way,"
and Jesus in our Gospel reading
confers on the church
the power to "bind and loose,"
the obligation to exercise judgement
and to hold people morally accountable
for their actions.
Our Scriptures recognize
that speaking out
may or may not prove to be effective
in changing someone's behavior,
but regardless of its effectiveness
we still have a moral obligation to speak,
we cannot keep the truth hidden
when it is under attack,
for if we do it is we who will be judged,
it is we who will be held accountable
for the evil we did not protest.

This past week the Catholic bishops
of the United States,
fulfilling their role
as successors to the apostles—
the role of binding and loosing,
of holding morally accountable—
issued a statement
in response to President Trump's cancellation
of the policy of Deferred Action for Childhood Arrivals.
This Obama-era policy allowed people who were
brought illegally to the United States as children
to remain in the country and to obtain work permits,

rather than being deported back
to countries of which they often have no memory,
and whose language they might not even speak.
The bishops, in their statement,
call the cancellation of this policy "reprehensible"
and say that such action represents
"a heartbreaking moment in our history
that shows the absence of mercy and good will,
and a short-sighted vision for the future."

Depending on the issue,
people on both the political left
and the political right
get annoyed
when the bishops do this sort of thing,
saying that the bishops are meddling in politics—
that they should stick to religion and the Bible
and leave politics to the politicians.
But it is precisely our religion
that compels us to speak up.
It is our sacred Scriptures that tell us that all people
are created in the image and likeness of God;
it is our sacred Scriptures that command us,
"You shall treat the alien who resides with you
no differently than the natives
born among you" (Leviticus 19:34);
it is Jesus Christ himself who says to us,
"I was hungry and you gave me no food,
I was thirsty and you gave me no drink,
a stranger and you gave me no welcome. . . .
I say to you, what you did not do
for one of these least ones,
you did not do for me" (Matthew 25:42–43, 45).

In speaking out, the bishops
are simply obeying God's command
to stand up for the weak and defend the defenseless,
to welcome Christ in welcoming the stranger,
to call the wandering to repentance.
Just as when they advocate for the unborn or the elderly,
just as when they denounce racism
or exploitation of the poor,
they are continuing the apostolic tradition
of prophetic protest against evil,
of binding and loosing and holding accountable.

You may be one of those people who, like me,
find yourself in the midst of such protest
saying, "I'm not sure that I entirely agree
with the precise wording of that sentiment,"
or, "Well, you know, the issue
is really a bit more complicated than this."
And it is true,
the details of immigration law and policy
are incredibly complicated.
But the heart of the gospel is not complicated:
"Owe nothing to anyone, except to love one another;
for the one who loves another has fulfilled the law. . . .
Love does no evil to the neighbor;
hence, love is the fulfillment of the law."

This law of love is simple, but it is not easy.
It demands that we come to see the world
through the eyes of Christ,
who fearlessly spoke the truth
and who laid down his life
out of love for us sinners.

It demands that we ourselves
love one another as he has loved us.
We love the oppressed
when we speak up
to denounce their oppression;
we love the oppressors
when we call them
to repentance and conversion;
we love the truth itself
when we refuse to let it be hidden
and give our lives to its service.

8. Inbound

46 *On Saturday, January 13, 2018, people in Hawaii received—via emergency alerts on phones, televisions, and radios—a message warning them of incoming missiles. I could not resist juxtaposing this event with Mark's account of Jesus's initial proclamation of the reign of God and the calling of his disciples, so as to wonder why Jesus's proclamation and call did not fill us with a sense of similar urgency. I am not sure the Gospel reading did much to illuminate this rather odd—and briefly terrifying—event, but perhaps the light that such an event casts on our lives and priorities might reveal something about our response or lack of response to the gospel.*

READINGS: Jonah 3:1–5, 10; 1 Corinthians 7:29–31;
Mark 1:16–20

There is nothing like
an impending ballistic missile strike
to focus the mind
and make us assess our priorities.
When the message went out
over the cell networks in Hawaii—
"Ballistic missile threat inbound to Hawaii.

Seek immediate shelter.
This is not a drill."—
I imagine people's priorities
got somewhat reshuffled.
I suspect people didn't stop
to update the apps on their phones
or check in for flights the next day.
I am pretty sure no one bothered
to switch the laundry from the washer to the dryer
or to clean the bathtub.
And I would be very surprised if anyone
checked to see how the market was doing
or what was up with the Kardashians.
But I do suspect that people
did things that might have otherwise
seemed to be trivial matters
that could be put off:
embracing loved ones,
letting go of long-standing grudges,
offering prayers to God
for mercy and protection.
There is something about the prospect
of a nuclear weapon hurtling toward you
that makes things you believe important
seem suddenly trivial,
and things you treat as trivial
seem suddenly urgent.

"Jesus came to Galilee
proclaiming the gospel of God:
'This is the time of fulfillment.
The kingdom of God is at hand.
Repent, and believe in the gospel.'"

Jesus is issuing the spiritual equivalent
of a warning about an incoming ballistic missile.
The drawing near of God's kingdom
causes us to reshuffle our priorities,
making important things trivial
and trivial things urgent.

In today's Gospel, our translation says
that when Jesus called Peter and Andrew,
"then they abandoned their nets and followed him,"
and that when he came across James and John,
"then he called them,
so they left their father Zebedee in the boat . . .
and followed him."
But a more literal translation
of the original Greek would be,
"*immediately* they abandoned their nets
and followed him,"
and "*immediately* he called them,
so they left their father Zebedee in the boat . . .
and followed him."

Now when a preacher begins talking to you
about the original Greek of the New Testament,
I generally think you are permitted
to let your eyes glaze over,
since you are likely in for
an irrelevant yet ostentatious
display of the thin veneer of learning
that people acquire in formation.
But in this case I ask you to indulge me.
For the Greek word that Mark uses here—*euthus*—
is one that he uses throughout his Gospel;

indeed, he uses it some forty times
in his sixteen short chapters
to propel his story forward with a sense of urgency.
Once the story begins, everything happens "immediately"
as Jesus hurtles toward his destiny in Jerusalem,
launched on a trajectory
that ends in cross and resurrection.
To be his follower is to be caught up
in that immediacy,
in that urgency,
which reshuffles our priorities,
so that possessions and work and even family
take second place to God's kingdom.
Peter and Andrew leave their boat and nets,
their very livelihood,
in order to follow Jesus.
James and John leave their father Zebedee behind
in order to be Jesus's disciples.

In our second reading, from Saint Paul,
we find a similar sense of urgency:
"The time is running out."
The preoccupations of this world—
family and possessions, joys and sorrows—
all look different in the light of the kingdom of God,
for, as Paul says,
"the world in its present form is passing away."
Paul's point is not, as some have suggested,
that Jesus is returning soon
and, therefore, we should focus our attention
on getting ready rather than on life in this world.
The point is rather that in Jesus
the kingdom has *already* drawn near

and the priorities and values of the world
are *already* in the process of passing away,
of being transformed
into the priorities and values of God's kingdom.
For Paul, no less than for Peter and Andrew,
or for James and John,
it is the call of Jesus to follow him
that makes "important" things trivial
and "trivial" things urgent.
Paul writes to the Philippians,

"I . . . consider everything as a loss
because of the supreme good
of knowing Christ Jesus my Lord.
For his sake I have accepted the loss of all things
and I consider them so much rubbish,
that I may gain Christ."

If you don't feel a certain urgency
in your life as a Christian,
you may have to ask yourself
whether you have truly understood
who Jesus Christ is.
If your response to Jesus's call to follow after him
does not involve a reshuffling of life's priorities,
you may want to ponder the words
of Dietrich Bonhoeffer,
the German theologian
who was executed by the Nazis:
"When Christ calls a person,
he bids them come and die."
If you do not see why
you need to respond immediately,

then you might want to listen again
to the words of Jesus:
"This is the time of fulfillment.
The kingdom of God is at hand."
Indeed, it is hurtling toward us,
making important things trivial
and trivial things urgent.

But, in addition to its sense
of immediacy and urgency,
the Gospel of Mark also has
a clear-eyed awareness
that those who sincerely desire
to be disciples of Jesus
often falter and fail,
that they let the priorities
and values of the world
deter them from following him
all the way to the cross,
that they do not yet know
in the deepest sense
who Jesus Christ is.
Yet the promise
with which Mark's Gospel ends,
that the risen Jesus has gone before us
and will meet us on the way,
is the promise that,
despite our faltering failures,
despite our misplaced priorities and values,
despite our blindness
to the presence of God's kingdom in Jesus,
God is merciful and forgiving and relentless.

The call to follow is renewed again and again,
and the kingdom is still at hand,
hurtling toward us on love's trajectory.
The risen Jesus still calls us:
This day is the time of fulfillment;
repent and believe in the gospel.

9. Hear, O Israel

The frequency of mass shootings can cause them all to blur to- 53
*gether in our minds. But of course each one is unique in some
way, not simply because of the unique lives snuffed out, but also
because of how these events are inflected by various ideologies and
motivations. The murders at the Tree of Life Synagogue on October 27, 2018, were motivated by the killer's noxious mix of white
nationalism, anti-immigrant sentiment, and anti-Semitism; he
saw President Donald Trump as controlled and manipulated by
the Jews around him. This somewhat eccentric ideology was fed
by a long history of anti-Semitism that has often drawn on distorted Christian theologies regarding the Jewish people. It seemed
the right moment to remind Christians of our ties to our elder
brothers and sisters in the faith.*

READINGS: Deuteronomy 6:2–6; Hebrews 7:23–28;
   Mark 12:28b–34

A little over a week after the murder
by an anti-Semitic white nationalist
of eleven worshippers
at the Tree of Life Synagogue in Pittsburgh,
our Scriptures remind us

of how much we Christians owe
to the Jewish people,
whom Pope John Paul II called
our elder brothers and sisters
in the faith of Abraham.
In our first reading,
from the book of Deuteronomy,
we hear the words of the Shema,
which has been described
as the closest thing Judaism has to a creed:
Sh'ma Yisra'eil Adonai Eloheinu Adonai echad—
"Hear, O Israel! The Lord is our God;
the Lord is one!"
And if God is one,
then we must love this God
not half-heartedly,
but with every fiber of our being:
"Therefore, you shall love
the Lord, your God,
with all your heart,
and with all your soul,
and with all your strength."
The one God demands of people
a single-hearted love.
Devout Jews recite the Shema each day
as part of their morning and evening prayers
to remind themselves of who God is
and who they are called to be.
The rabbis called the act of reciting the Shema
"receiving the yoke
of the kingdom of heaven"
(*Berakhot Mishnah* 2:5);
to say these words is to commit oneself

to the joyful task of bearing the burden
of faith in the one God.

In today's Gospel reading,
the words of the Shema are quoted by Jesus
in response to the scribe's question,
"Which is the first of all the commandments?"
We can presume that Jesus, as a devout Jew,
had these words on his lips twice daily,
so he probably did not have to ponder too long
as to what was the first and greatest commandment.
And he probably did not have to ponder too long
before adding as the second commandment
words from the book of Leviticus:
"You shall love your neighbor as yourself."
For this too is fundamental to Judaism:
love of God and love of neighbor—
the first and second tables of the Law—
are inextricably linked.
Jesus bore within himself the faith of Israel,
and as members of his body
we too bear this faith,
we too receive the joyful yoke
of the kingdom of heaven.

I do not want to minimize the theological differences
between Christians and Jews.
Christians, for example, interpret the oneness of God
that the Shema proclaims
in such a way as to include the divine threeness
of Father, Son, and Spirit—
a notion that Jews generally find odd, to say the least.
And, as we hear today in the Letter to the Hebrews,

Christians ascribe to Jesus an eternal priesthood,
seeing in his death and resurrection
the source of the world's salvation,
another notion that Jews find odd, to say the least.
But our honest acknowledgement of such differences
must not blind us to what we share:
faith in the one God, who is the God of all peoples;
the command to love this God with undivided love;
and the knowledge that love of God calls us
to love our neighbor as we love ourselves.
We too must each day and night
take up the yoke of the kingdom of heaven.

The murders at the Tree of Life synagogue
were not only a human horror,
but they also did violence to our common faith.
This act assaulted the idea that God is one God,
caring and providing for everyone on earth.
It trampled on the idea of single-hearted love of God
by desecrating the Sabbath worship of God's people.
It slaughtered the command to love our neighbor
as we love ourselves.
It shattered the yoke of the kingdom of God.

How do we respond to such violence and hatred?
Not with our own retaliatory hatred,
but with the love that the Shema commands,
and with a renewed commitment
to this common faith.
This violence can only be repaired by God,
but we remind ourselves day and night
of this God, to whom we owe single-hearted love,
and of the neighbor whom we love

for the sake of this God.
We should recite these words
before reading the news or casting a vote.
We should teach these words to our children
until they are written on their hearts.
We should constantly ask ourselves
what our lives ought to look like
if we truly love the one God with all our heart
and with all our soul
and with all our strength,
and if we truly love our neighbor as ourselves.

If we take upon our shoulders
the joyful yoke of this common faith,
perhaps Jesus will say to us
what he said to the scribe:
"You are not far from the kingdom of God."
Sh'ma Yisra'eil Adonai Eloheinu Adonai echad.

10. Insurrection

THE BAPTISM OF THE LORD

JANUARY 10, 2021

58   *In the summer of 2019 I was transferred to the Cathedral of Mary Our Queen (see homily 37), where there is a much wider array of political opinion than left-leaning Corpus Christi Church. While not engaging in self-censorship, I realized that a more politically diverse audience might require a lighter touch. But the assault on the Capitol on January 6, 2021, required, I thought, a very direct response, particularly regarding the role played by President Donald Trump. Simply lamenting division would not do. Afterward, I received a number of appreciative remarks from parishioners, but also a few negative ones, including a couple of people accusing me of hypocrisy (I eventually persuaded them that what they were really accusing me of was not hypocrisy but lying). This event has made clear to me that, while preaching should not set out to be divisive, the preaching of the gospel will sometimes uncover division, and preachers must be willing to pay the cost of doing this. In my case, the cost was a few insults; others have paid much higher costs.*

READINGS: Isaiah 55:1–11; 1 John 5:1–9; Mark 1:7–11

I had a very nice homily in mind for today:
something about ancient Israelite cosmology
and the symbolic role it plays in Mark's story

of Jesus's baptism.
But, as so often happens in life and ministry,
events interrupt our plans,
and I feel compelled to say something
about the assault on the Capitol building
and about what light the gospel of Jesus Christ
can shed in these dark days.

I feel compelled to say something,
but I speak with trepidation,
since I cannot really say anything
about these things
without saying something
about the role played by our president.
I know that fifty percent of Catholics
who voted in the last election
voted for Mr. Trump—
for a variety of reasons, of course,
and with varying degrees of enthusiasm.
Still, odds are that some of you
might not like what I must say.
But say it I must,
so I hope you will hear me out.

It is hard to deny that this past Wednesday
the words of President Trump were a spark,
falling upon the fuel
of weeks of unsubstantiated
and repeatedly debunked claims
of a stolen election,
a spark that ignited an insurrection that led
to an attempt by some to derail
the peaceful transfer of power

and ultimately to the deaths of five people.
The resignations of numerous people
from Mr. Trump's administration make it evident
that even the most ardent supporters of his policies
have been forced to recognize his role
in inciting these shameful and deadly actions.
Even those who rejoice in his support
for the pro-life movement
have been forced to see in his actions
a blatant disregard
for the sanctity of life and for the common good.

I will admit that his words and actions
have made me angry.
But they have also made me profoundly sad.
They have made me sad because I see in Mr. Trump
a dark truth about human beings in general.
Donald Trump, despite some residual bluster,
now stands defeated—
not by circumstances,
not by his political foes,
not by the media,
but ultimately by himself.
He has been defeated by an aversion to truth
that all of us in our own ways share.
I do not know if his false claim
to have won the election by a landslide
is a cynical deception or a sincere delusion,
but whether deception or delusion
it is certainly evidence of something
that is true of all of us to some extent,
whatever our political persuasion:
In our desire for mastery over our lives,

and the lives of others,
we will believe and promote falsehoods;
we will deny and suppress the truth
to bolster our egos,
even when doing so deadens our souls
and harms those around us.
As the poet T. S. Eliot put it,
"Humankind cannot bear very much reality."

You see this aversion to reality in Scripture,
in the story of our first parents,
who chose to believe the serpent's lies
that they could steal the wisdom of God
and so become the source and meaning
of their own existence.
You see it today in the allure
of elaborate conspiracy theories that we embrace
because they support our worldview.
You see it in our resistance to new information
that might challenge our beliefs or lifestyles.
You see it in the tenacity with which we cling
to the conviction that our side, our party, our tribe
should be completely identified with the forces of light
and that those who disagree or oppose us
must be cast as the forces of darkness.

To recognize in Mr. Trump something that is,
to one degree or another,
true of all of us
is not to excuse his actions.
He had a choice,
just as we all have a choice.
We have a choice

because into the darkness
of deception and delusion
a light has shone,
and the darkness has not overcome it.
When Christ is baptized,
the heavens are torn open
and the Spirit of truth descends upon him
and, through him, is unleashed upon our world.
Writing of Christ's baptism,
Saint Gregory of Nazianzus said,

"Christ is bathed in light; let us also be bathed in light."
Christ did not go down
into the waters of the River Jordan
in order to be cleansed of sin,
but rather to purify the dark stream of human blindness
that flows from the sin of our first parents.
He plunges into the waters of deception and delusion
to transform them into waters of light and life.

In these enlightening waters we find
not just our salvation,
but an invitation, a call, a summons
to reflect in the world the light of truth
that has shone upon us.
Saint Gregory writes, "God wants you
to become a living force for all humanity,
lights shining in the world.
You are to be radiant lights
as you stand beside Christ,
the great light,
bathed in the glory of him
who is the light of heaven."
We must live as light in a world of lies.

We must first and foremost proclaim the great truth
of the world's redemption through Christ,
but we must also guard the more ordinary truths
from which our daily common life is woven.
We must resist the impulse to believe and promote
falsehoods that offer our egos
temporary comfort in the illusion of mastery.
We must bear witness to the truth,
even when that truth discomfits us,
because without truth we are doomed.

We have seen this week one more example
of the destructive force of deception and delusion,
and we have heard in our Gospel a call
to be bathed in the Spirit of truth.
May Christ our way heal and bless our country,
may Christ our truth enlighten and empower his church,
and may Christ our life have mercy on us all.

PART 2

Culture Happens

Part of the power of Jesus's parables in their original context is how they used culturally familiar figures— shepherds and landowners—and activities—hiring day laborers and traveling a dangerous road—to depict the nature of God's mysterious reign, often twisting the familiar into the unfamiliar and trading on the shock value of overturning cultural assumptions. In Jesus's day, there was no such thing as "popular culture." There was just "culture": the shared ways of getting through life, the common fund of stories and songs, the manners and expectations that made life together possible. But in the modern world we have an entertainment industry making cultural artifacts for our consumption, as well as seemingly unplanned cultural phenomena that spread like viruses (the original sense of "meme," as the term was coined by Richard Dawkins), or past events that have become cultural monuments to be recalled on an annual basis. And preachers often feel that they should make use of such cultural phenomena, just as Jesus did.

No less than when engaging current events, a preacher engaging some aspect of popular culture runs a number of risks. Practically speaking, we live in an era of fragmented popular culture, with ever more finely sliced niche markets, so it is quite possible that whatever cultural reference we make will be unfamiliar to a majority of our listeners. Also, many of us religious types are not particularly well plugged in culture-wise, and we risk coming across as lame panderers as we awkwardly discuss the latest cultural phenomenon (is there anything more cringe-inducing than a fortysomething preacher talking about some TikTok video?). Then there is the danger of suggesting that the gospel needs some sort of validation via relevance, as if we are tacitly acknowledging that Jesus isn't nearly as interesting as the latest superhero movie.

But like the news cycle, popular culture is worth engaging. This is particularly so in those increasingly rare cases when there is some cultural phenomenon that is widely known, that everyone present can connect to in some way or other. It may also happen that some bit of popular culture has a connection to the gospel that is particularly pointed or challenging, or that something happening in the wider cultural milieu is of specific relevance to the particular congregation. In such cases, I feel justified—at times even compelled—to let popular culture into my preaching.

11. Superheroes

This is the most egregious example of pop culture exploitation   67
in this collection, and in some ways the least successful, since it
*referenced a recent movie—*The Amazing Spider-Man, *starring*
Andrew Garfield—that many in the congregation had not yet
seen. I think the homily still made its point even for those who had
not seen the movie, and I mainly referenced the movie because
I was quite taken by the villain's stated desire for a "world without
weakness." But perhaps the same themes could have been framed
differently. As it turned out, there was a visiting youth group
present that Sunday, so we had a larger number of young peo-
ple than usual, but none of them seemed particularly impressed
by my Spider-Man knowledge. Still, I think the homily worked
well enough, perhaps because its point concerning weakness could
stand on its own, without the support of Spider-Man.

READINGS: Ezekiel 2:2–5; 2 Corinthians 12:7–10;
  Mark 6:1–6

I don't typically look
to summer blockbusters or superheroes
for the starting point of a homily,
but in light of today's readings

I could not help but think
of the new reboot of *Spider-Man*
that debuted this past week.
The villain in the movie,
the one-armed mad scientist Dr. Curt Connors,
is driven to harness the regenerative power of reptiles—
you know, the way that lizards can regrow their tails—
not only so that he can regrow his own missing arm
but so that he might create, as he puts it,
"a world without weakness."

Well, as usually happens to mad scientists,
Dr. Connors's ambitions involve him
in some serious technological overreach and
(spoiler alert!)
he ends up turning himself
into a giant reptilian monster
and terrorizing New York City
until Spider-Man comes along
to save the day.

As I said, I don't usually look for wisdom from movies,
particularly not from ones
in which the main character dresses in spandex,
but in this case I think that,
in addition to some awesome 3D special effects,
we have a genuine insight:
our desire to create a world without weakness,
no matter how well intentioned it may seem,
will in the end destroy our humanity
because in this life
weakness is part of our human condition.

It was the rhetoric of ridding the world of weakness
that accompanied Hitler's murderous campaign
to cleanse the world of so-called inferior races.
It is perhaps a desire for a world without weakness
that accounts for the fact
that at least 70 percent of pregnancies
in which the fetus is diagnosed with Down syndrome
are terminated.
It is the quest for what we might call
"a church without weakness"
that leads some to desire a smaller, "purer" church,
presumably one that is rid of all those
who might struggle with the teachings of the church
on various matters of faith and morals.
And it is the desire for a self without weakness
that leads us either to deny our own frailty,
or to loathe the frailty within ourselves
that we cannot deny.

Our second reading,
from Paul's Second Letter to the Corinthians,
is one of the New Testament's
most profound reflections
on the grace of living
in a world of weakness.
Paul says that God gave him
a "thorn in the flesh,
an angel [or 'messenger'] of Satan"—
in order to remind him of his weakness.
This might refer to a physical disability
or perhaps to some sort of moral temptation
to which Paul was prone,

but whatever the nature of this "thorn,"
when Paul prays three times to have it removed
God says in reply, "My grace is sufficient for you,
for power is made perfect in weakness."

Power is made perfect in weakness.
Saint Thomas Aquinas comments
that this is "a remarkable way of speaking,"
sort of like saying
"fire increases in water."

But this remarkable way of speaking
should be, for we who are Christians,
our native language
because it allows us
to speak eloquently of God's grace.
If we boast of our weakness—
if we acknowledge our fragility—
then, Paul tells us,
the power of Christ will dwell in us.
The power of Christ is not a power
that makes a world without weakness
but rather a power that makes its dwelling
within our world of weakness,
a power that inhabits weakness
in order to offer a way through weakness
into God's embrace.
The cross shows us
the perfection of power in weakness
in all its mystery,
for it is our faith as Christians
that through the cross of Jesus
God has poured out the power of grace,
a grace abundant to save an entire world of weakness.

And when we know our own weakness we are set free
to embrace the very power of God.

Accepting our own weakness
we are also set free to accept
the weakness of others,
to give up our dream
of the perfect spouse or child,
our dream of the perfect church,
our dream of a world without weakness.
To know your own weakness
is to have God's Spirit
open your heart to others
in compassion and mercy.

What is your weakness?
What is the thorn in your flesh?
In a sense, it doesn't matter.
What matters
is that we *all* live in a world of weakness.
What matters
is that God invites us today to know our weakness
so that we may know fully
the power of God's grace at work in us.
We should not seek a world without weakness,
for when we are weak—
when we know our own helplessness
and our need for mercy—
it is then we are strong in mercy
through the power of God.

12. The Mayan Calendar

72 *Because they are so numerous, it is difficult to recall all the various predictions of the world's end that have crossed our path, but the Mayan calendar was a big deal. They even made a fairly terrible blockbuster movie based on the supposed fact that the Mayan calendar ran out in 2012 (it didn't, but that didn't stop people). The poor Mayan calendar got many flakey pseudoscientific claims attached to it, and it was quite a bit of fun to mock the whole affair, not least because for once it wasn't some apocalyptic Christian sect predicting the world's demise. But amid all the mocking, I thought it was important to reflect on why it is that people might not just predict but actively long for the world's ending, and how this somewhat exotic desire might be related to our own desires for a more just and peaceful world.*

READINGS: Jeremiah 33:14–16; 1 Thessalonians 3:12–4:2; Luke 21:25–28, 34–36

Advent is a season of expectation:
a time of expectant preparation
for our celebration of Christ's birth
two thousand years ago,
for the coming of Christ into our lives today,

and for the glorious return of Christ on the last day.
This Sunday our attention is drawn particularly
to Christ's future coming in glory:
"There will be signs in the sun, the moon, and the stars,
and on earth nations will be in dismay,
perplexed by the roaring of the sea and the waves."

Of course, this year things are a little bit different,
since this year we know that
when the ancient Mayan calendar runs out
on December 21, 2012,
the end of the world is upon us,
whether it is caused by a black hole eating up the earth
or a collision between the earth
and the mysterious planet Nibiru.
And I've got to say that knowing this
certainly simplifies things in my life.
I've told my daughter Sophie
to forget about getting those college applications done,
and I'm thinking about canceling
the repairs on our leaking roof.

Speculation and prediction
about when the world will end
is not really something unique to this year
and to enthusiasts of the Mayan calendar.
Last year the radio preacher Harold Camping
predicted that the world would end on May 21, 2011;
and when May 21 came and went,
he revised that to October 21.
Prior to that, various groups and individuals
had predicted the end of the world in
1889, 1874, 1844, 1763, 1585, 1533, 1370,

1284, 1260, 1033, 1000, 992, 793, 500.
In fact, I think we can safely presume
that pretty much *every* year
has been a candidate for the world's end
in somebody's calculation.

I must admit that
I don't take end of the world speculations very seriously,
and I suspect this is true of many of you as well.
But a lot of people do, so it is worth asking:

What is it that attracts people to such speculations?

I suppose that we might take
a negative attitude toward them
and say that they are an expression of our human desire
for control over our own destinies,
a desire to put God on a timetable
that we can plan around.
This is certainly part of what is going on,
and it is why the preacher Harold Camping
has recently denounced his own attempts
to predict the date of the world's end as "sinful."

But I don't think such predictions are *only*
manifestations of a sinful desire for control.
I think that they are also a sign
that one is living one's life
in expectant hope of deliverance.
Those who look for this world's ending
seem to be those who have a profound sense
that something is wrong with this world,
marked as it is by sin and death,
and that we await a deliverer who will set things right,

who will "do what is right and just in the land."
Perhaps people come up with dates for this world's end
because they yearn so fervently for a world where,
as our first reading says, we can "dwell secure."
In other words,
perhaps those most interested in the world's end
are those whose lives in this world are most insecure,
whether materially, socially, emotionally, or spiritually.
And perhaps people like me,
who tend to dismiss end of the world speculations,
might have something to learn
from those who take them seriously—
not their predictions that the world will end
on this or that date,
but the fundamental and undeniable truth
that my life *is* in fact insecure,
that the life that I have so carefully constructed
could collapse in an instant,
through sickness, unemployment, betrayal, or death.
The one thing that does seem secure
is that *my* world, *my* life, will end.
Perhaps what I need to learn is that,
as Jesus says in today's Gospel,
my heart has grown drowsy
with the concerns of everyday life
so that I overlook
the fundamental insecurity and fragility
of my very existence—
not to mention the suffering of those
whose lives are far more insecure than mine:
the poor and the dispossessed.

To wake up to this insecurity is also, by God's grace,

to awaken to an expectant hope for a savior
in whose love I can dwell secure.
The message of the gospel
is ultimately not about the insecurity of this life,
but about the security of the love of God
that comes to us in Jesus Christ,
the love that allows us to face life's insecurities with hope,
knowing our redemption is at hand in every moment.
Because of the love that God has shown us in Jesus
we can look in hope beyond our insecurity,

not to a fixed date on which the world will end,
but to the certain advent in our lives
of the God who is love
and whose love will one day
be fully manifest in our world.

13. The Reckless Shepherd

Knowledge of sheep is not particularly common in our culture—so much so that we fail to notice the somewhat bizarre behavior of the shepherd in Jesus's parable of the lost sheep. But an event emblazoned in the memory of every American over twenty-five is the terrorist attacks of September 11, 2001. Commemoration of this event has become a cultural monument, at the heart of which we remember not merely the tragic deaths of those who died simply because they had shown up for work in the wrong place at the wrong time, but also the genuinely heroic deaths of the firefighters, paramedics, and police officers who died while trying to rescue people. In this homily, preached on the fifteenth anniversary of those attacks, I point to those first responders as showing us something of what is going on in Jesus's parable.

READINGS: Exodus 32:7–11, 13–14; 1 Timothy 1:12–17;
Luke 15:1–10

Jesus begins his parable with a question:
"What man among you
having a hundred sheep and losing one of them
would not leave the ninety-nine in the desert
and go after the lost one until he finds it?"

Jesus is being his usual tricky self here,
making it sound as if what he is proposing
is obviously reasonable,
when in fact *nobody* with an ounce of shepherding sense
would leave ninety-nine sheep alone in the desert
in order to look for a single missing one.
Even the most basic form of risk assessment
would tell you that this is a very, very, very bad idea.

We find a version of this parable
in the second-century document
known as the Gospel of Thomas,
which tries to make this very, very, very bad idea
sound a bit more reasonable
by noting that the lost sheep is the largest of the flock,
and also by having the shepherd
tell the sheep when he finds it,
"I love you more than the ninety-nine" (*logion* 107),
suggesting that this is somehow a very special sheep.
But the parable as we find it in sacred Scripture
gives no such indication, makes no such excuse
for the shepherd's professional irresponsibility.
The only thing special about the sheep is that it is lost
and the other ninety-nine are not.

We might forgive the author of the Gospel of Thomas
for trying to make Jesus's parable
a little less offensive to common sense,
a little less foolish.
But honesty requires that we recognize
that if we measure the shepherd's behavior
by our ordinary human standards
it really doesn't make much sense.

This is why the fifth-century bishop Peter Chrysologus,
who perhaps knew something about actual shepherding,
noted, "This story . . . speaks of no earthly shepherd
but of a heavenly one,
and far from being a portrayal of human activity,
this whole parable conceals divine mysteries"
(Sermon 168).
It is not a lesson in animal husbandry
but in the mystery of divine love:
a love that might seem foolish by human standards,
a love that squanders security on a risky venture,
a love that favors the lost one
no matter how seemingly unimportant that lost one is.
This is the God revealed in Jesus Christ,
the God who, our second reading tells us,
"came into the world to save sinners."
Jesus presents the shepherd's foolish action
as if it were completely reasonable
because, as Saint Paul says,
the foolishness of God
is wiser than human wisdom,
and the weakness of God
is stronger than human strength (1 Corinthians 1:25).

For most of us today, parables about shepherds
might not seem to have much in the way
of immediate relevance.
Perhaps if we want to grasp
the reckless foolishness
of divine love seeking the lost one
we need new parables.
On this anniversary
of the terrorist attacks of 2001,

I cannot help but think
of those first responders in New York,
police and firefighters
who ran back into the burning, collapsing towers
to try to bring out those
who were lost within an inferno
that fear and hatred had created.
Over four hundred of them lost their lives that day
in what some might call acts of heroism,
but which others might see
as foolish and reckless missions
with little or no hope of success.

But we who seek to be followers of Jesus
ought to see in their actions
neither pointless sacrifice
nor even mere heroic bravery
but a parable of God made flesh in Jesus,
the divine lover who comes to seek the lost one,
even at the cost of his own life.
For we believe that in Jesus Christ
God ran headlong into the inferno of our world,
an inferno kindled by sin's fear and hatred
and within which we were lost.
He took upon himself the suffering of the cross
in order to find us
in the midst of the world's pain and chaos
and to bring us forth
into the dawning light of his resurrection.
And through the grace of his Spirit Jesus continues
to enter into the disasters of our lives—
the disasters we make by our choices

or which fortune forces upon us—
to find us and bring us home to God.
Into the pain and chaos and tragedy of my life
Jesus comes to rescue *me*,
not because I am the best,
not because I am special,
but simply because I am lost.

Both the reckless shepherd of whom Jesus speaks
and the heroic first responders of September 11
should be parables to us
of the relentless, foolish, risky,
but ultimately triumphant love
that God has for the lost one,
the love that led Jesus
through the cross to the resurrection.
But the shepherd,
the heroes of 9/11,
and the cross of Christ
should also stand as a challenge to us.
In coming to seek us in our lostness,
in bringing us out
into the light of his resurrection,
Jesus calls and empowers us with his Spirit
to become sharers in his ministry of reconciliation.
He calls us to seek the lost one,
even if our efforts seem unlikely
to yield success as the world sees it.
He calls us to enter into
the inferno of fear and hatred
that sin has made of our world,
with faith that the grace of God

will find a way to use us
to speak a word of hope,
to perform an act of love,
to risk opening up our lives
so that *we* become parables
of the relentless, foolish, risky,
but ultimately triumphant love of God.

14. The Keepers

I have preached a lot on the sex abuse catastrophe in the Catholic   **83**
Church, not least because the church has offered ample occasion.
This collection includes only three of many homilies I have given
on the topic (this one, as well as homilies 16 and 20), in part
because I generally always say the same sorts of things. This par-
ticular homily was occasioned by two cultural events: the #MeToo
movement, particularly as it exposed powerful men in the enter-
tainment industry, and the widely watched Netflix documentary
The Keepers, *which told the story of sexual abuse in a Balti-*
more Catholic high school in the late 1960s. The Keepers *was,*
I thought, aesthetically flawed—far too long and larded with
schlocky and anachronistic Catholic imagery—but the story itself
was filled with horrifying power, especially since I knew some of
the people who appeared on camera. The convergence of these two
events prompted me to reflect on the abuse of power among those
who tell the stories from which we draw meaning.

READINGS: Malachi 1:14b–2:2b, 8–10;
   1 Thessalonians 2:7b–9, 13; Matthew 23:1–12

In the 1930s a theater critic is purported to have said,
"Theaters are the new Church of the Masses—

where people sit huddled in the dark
listening to people in the light
tell them what it is to be human."
To be in a position to tell people
what it is to be human
is to be invested with immense,
almost godlike power—
power that can be easily abused.
And in recent weeks, we have been confronted
with an unending stream of news stories

of sexual abuse and harassment
by powerful men in the entertainment industry.
Each day seems to bring new allegations,
showing that such behavior is not rare but pervasive.

We Catholics have lived for at least the past fifteen years
with the depressingly frequent experience
of being smacked in the face by the failures of our clergy,
particularly the repeated revelations
of sexual abuse of children and young people
by priests, deacons, and religious.
Most recently,
the Netflix documentary series *The Keepers*
has chronicled in horrifying detail
the widespread abuse of girls by a priest
who worked as a counselor in the late '60s and early '70s
at Keough High School here in Baltimore.
Even if, as the archdiocese claims,
The Keepers is somewhat misleading
in its portrayal of the archdiocese's response
to the allegations of abuse,
nobody seriously questions the truth
of the allegations themselves

or the way in which
the religious authority of the priesthood
was used to enable horrific acts of abuse.

It is a powerful thing to be in the position
of telling people what it means to be human,
whether it is done in a church or in a theater,
and the exercise of such power
is seductive and intoxicating.
And make no mistake, these cases of abuse,
whether by priests or producers or political pundits,
are about power, not sexual desire.
They are about the thrill of having someone
totally in your control,
the titillation found
in bending someone's will to your own,
the ancient human delusion
that one exercises godlike power over others
because one has the authority
to declare the meaning of human existence.
And the fact that the meaning of human existence
proclaimed by the church is true
doesn't make the abuse of power by the clergy better;
in fact, it makes it worse.
It becomes not only a violation of human dignity
but a perversion of the truth of God.

The seduction of religious or quasi-religious power
is not, of course, anything new.
Jesus identifies it in the religious leaders of his own day:
"They preach, but they do not practice. . . .
They love places of honor at banquets,
seats of honor in synagogues,

greetings in the marketplace."
These things might seem comparatively minor
compared to violent acts of abuse,
but they grow from the same poisoned root.
In Jesus's day, as in ours,
the power to proclaim
the meaning of human existence
is quickly and easily twisted
into a tool for domination.

86 But what does Jesus say?
"The greatest among you must be your servant.
Whoever exalts himself will be humbled;
but whoever humbles himself will be exalted."
And Jesus doesn't just speak this truth, he lives it;
he lives it to the point of death, death on a cross.
And in that life, in that death,
not only the meaning of human existence
but the true power of God is revealed.
In our quest for godlike power,
we not only mistake ourselves for God
but we also mistake the nature of God's power.
God's power as revealed in the cross
is not a power over others
that allows God to control and manipulate
in order to enhance and increase his own sense of power.
Rather God's power is one that constantly pours itself out
in creating, in healing, in forgiving,
in giving itself to be shared in.
We truthfully proclaim
the meaning of human existence
when we exercise power in this way,

the way that Jesus reveals
in his life, death, and resurrection.

Writing to the Thessalonians,
Paul gives us a picture of such a proclamation:
"We were gentle among you,
as a nursing mother cares for her children. . . .
Working night and day
in order not to burden any of you,
we proclaimed to you the gospel of God."
Paul uses the image of the nursing mother
who shares her own bodily substance with her child
to speak of the nature of true religious authority.
How different this is from those exercises
of religious or quasi-religious power
that find their end in self-gratification
through control and manipulation.

Those of us who are clergy
ought to look to Jesus and Paul
to teach us how to proclaim the good news.
We cannot let the abuses of power
by those who are called to proclaim
the meaning of human existence
cause us to cease our proclamation.
Because the world still needs the good news of God,
and there are plenty of peddlers of other gospels
waiting to step into the breach should we fall silent.
We must find a way to proclaim that good news
as Jesus did, as Paul did,
not only with our lips but in our lives,
so that those who receive it may find, as Paul says,

"not a human word but . . . the word of God,
which is now at work in you who believe."

When I was ordained a deacon,
Archbishop Keeler
placed the book of Gospels in my hands,
saying, "Receive the gospel of Christ
whose herald you have become.
Believe what you read,
teach what you believe,
and practice what you teach."
This is an awesome charge.
To fulfill it,
I need you to hold me accountable
in exercising the kind of authority
that does not exalt itself
and does not seek its own advantage,
but seeks only to build up the body of Christ
here in this place.
I also need you to pray for me,
to pray for all bishops, priests, and deacons,
that we may have the power to be gentle,
the power to proclaim what it means to be human
by seeking no glory except the glory of the cross.

PART 3

Church Life

Preaching that is attentive to news cycles and popular culture looks outward at events in the world through the eyes of the gospel—as Barth put it, interpreting the news through the Bible, or as the Second Vatican Council put it, "scrutinizing the signs of the times and . . . interpreting them in the light of the Gospel" (*Gaudium et Spes* §4). But sometimes we must be attentive to what is happening *within* the church or on the borderline *between* the church and the world.

Like all preaching that does not seek to occupy a vantage point removed from the particular, focusing on intraecclesial happenings entails risk. Those who are present in church on a typical Sunday are most likely to be "churchy" people, by which I mean those who have been formed by the church and who, to one degree or another, find what is going on in the church somewhat interesting. Too much focus on events in the church—whether controversies or conclaves or canonizations—can end up alienating the nonchurchy people, the seekers who have shown up looking for solace, looking for Jesus, and find themselves in the midst of what sounds like a discussion of inside baseball. Likewise, it can foster in the churchy people an unhealthy obsession with ecclesiastical politics, with pet positions of their particular faction, or with theological trivia that obscures the heart of the gospel.

But not every glance in a mirror turns one into Narcissus. While we should avoid suggesting that the church is somehow more interesting than Jesus, the church does in fact have a life she lives, a life that flows from the Spirit living within her, and that life must be attended to. There are specific teachings that must be conveyed, specific intentions that must be prayed for, specific events that must be reflected on. To put it another way, the people of the church need to find ways of being firmly rooted in the church without being superficially churchy, and it is part of the task of preaching to help them do this.

15. The Gospel of Life

Since 1972, Roman Catholics in the United States have taken
the first Sunday of October as an occasion to focus on respect for
human life, from conception to natural death. The parish where
I was first assigned as a deacon had the reputation as one of the
"liberal" parishes in the diocese. Among other things, what this
meant was that we did not talk much about the issue of abortion.
So it was with some trepidation that I, only recently ordained,
gave this homily—trying to speak truthfully without stridency.
At the church door afterward I received some mild pushback, as
well as remarks suggesting grudging respect for my willingness
to address the topic. But that evening I received a call at home
from a parishioner who was a long-standing pillar of the parish
as well as a medical professional. I half expected her to tell me
that I had no idea what I was talking about and had no right
to speak on the issue. Instead she said that she had been waiting
years to hear that homily and she wanted to thank me for it. So
you just never know.

READINGS: Genesis 2:18–24; Hebrews 2:9–11; Mark 10:2–16

Today is designated
by the Church in the United States

as "Respect Life Sunday."
The phrase "respect for life"
is not simply a code word
for the issue of abortion.
Catholic teaching on respect for life extends to issues
of poverty, health care, war, the death penalty,
the environment, the disabled, and so forth.
As Eileen Egan put it,
"The protection of life is a seamless garment.
You can't protect some lives and not others."

I would like to think that part of the strength
of our tradition of Catholic Social Teaching
is precisely the breadth of vision that is involved
when we speak of respect for life.

But I also think it is worth focusing at times
on respect for human life
at its earliest stages of development
not least because many Catholics
feel confused and conflicted
over how to think about this issue,
feeling as if they are being presented by our culture
with the demand that we choose
between concern for the unborn
and concern for women.
Catholic teaching about respect for life
says that this is a false choice.
But the only way that we will begin to see
another way of framing the issue
is if we begin with what, for Christians,
is the most fundamental question:
What does Jesus Christ require of us?

In today's Gospel, we hear that Jesus
welcomed the children
who were brought to him;
he blessed them, and told his disciples that
"the kingdom of God
belongs to such as these,"
going on to say that
"whoever does not accept
the kingdom of God like a child
will not enter it."
Jesus seems to be saying that those
who inherit the kingdom of God
are those who, like children,
are without power, without strength,
and who must rely entirely on others—
who must rely entirely on God.
Those who are weak and vulnerable
have a privileged place within our community
because they are living signs of who we must become
if we wish to enter God's reign.
As Catholics, our concern for the unborn
does not grow primarily
from a right to life that they possess,
but from the fact that we cannot be
the people whom God calls us to be
unless we protect and foster the lives of those
who are least able to care for themselves,
unless we see the unique beauty and value
that grows from that vulnerability,
unless we extend to the most vulnerable
the same welcome that Jesus himself did.
To be who we are called to be

as members of Christ's body,
we must care for the unborn.

This is something distinct,
though not separable,
from the legal and political controversy
surrounding the issue of abortion.
In our Gospel reading today
Jesus treats the question
put to him by the Pharisees
about the Jewish laws
concerning marriage and divorce
as rather beside the point
when thinking about how his followers
should approach these matters.
Jesus says that Moses gave them that law,
"because of the hardness of your hearts"—
to establish a minimum standard of semijustice—
not as the standard by which
we measure Christian discipleship.
If this is true of the law given by God through Moses,
how much more true it is of our human laws.
Any legal structure will be at best
a distant approximation of the justice that God desires.

This does not mean that our laws are unimportant;
indeed, with regard to the issue of abortion
I think every Catholic should desire
that our nation's laws would foster and protect
the lives of the unborn.
But, unlike some, I also think
that the exact nature of those laws,
and how they would relate to other goods

that need fostering and protection,
and how distantly or closely
they might approximate true justice,
are matters over which it is possible
for Catholics to differ in good faith.
I have my own ideas about these matters,
and I am sure that many of you do as well,
and it might be interesting to discuss these sometime,
preferably over a drink, or maybe three.

But the political question, important as it is,
cannot be for us the first question.
The first question is not one of legislation
or court decisions
or executive orders;
it is the question,
what should we as the church of Jesus Christ
do to help create a world
in which every child is welcomed
and cared for from the moment of conception,
and recognized as one of the "little ones"
whom Christ himself welcomes?

In asking this question,
we see that our concern for these children
is inseparable from a concern
for the mothers of these children.
This is part of the reason why in Catholic teaching
the respect for life is a seamless garment.
We can't separate the issue of abortion
from the fight against poverty
or the fight for the dignity of women.
Our concern for the unborn

must extend to the material needs
of women who are pregnant
in difficult circumstances,
and this is an area in which individual Catholics
as well as numerous Catholic social service agencies
have an admirable record,
though there is of course always more that can be done.

But our concern must extend beyond material needs.
We have a gospel—good news—to share,
what Pope John Paul II called "The Gospel of Life."
And part of the message of this gospel
is that even when it appears that there is no way forward,
when we can see no good choices,
when we seem trapped by circumstances,
we can have faith that God can make a way forward,
and with the help of God's grace and God's people
God can strengthen us to choose life.

People often see the abortion issue
in terms of tragic choices,
and I would never want
to underestimate the moral struggle
of women who find themselves pregnant
in difficult circumstances,
or to suggest that choosing life
does not often require women
to live lives of heroic virtue.
Choosing life might mean raising a child
when you are young or single or poor.
Choosing life might mean caring for a disabled child
long past his or her childhood, into adulthood.
Choosing life might mean living

with the lifelong sense of loss
experienced by many women
who surrender their children for adoption.
These are heroic choices.
But the gospel tells us that God's grace
makes such heroism possible,
if we can receive that grace
with the trust of a child
and if God's church is ready
to be the kind of community
that will itself go to heroic lengths
to be a place where such heroic choices
can be lived out.
The gospel also tells us
that when we fail to live heroically,
there is mercy and forgiveness
to be found in God's church.

For Christians, there are no tragic dead ends
because the world's story is ultimately not a tragedy
that ends with the bodies of the dead
strewn across the stage of history,
with nothing left to do but the work of mourning.
Rather, for Christians the world's story ends
with the marriage of heaven and earth
and the wedding feast of the Lamb.
This is the vision that we have to offer to the world:
a vision that sees beauty in vulnerability,
a vision that we possess only to the degree
that we actually put it into practice.
This is the vision that must sustain our hope
that our respect for life
can weave together concern for the unborn

and concern for women,
together with concern for the poor, the elderly,
the disabled, and the imprisoned,
into a seamless garment in which we,
as Christ's body,
can be clothed
as we bear witness
to the Gospel of Life in our world.

16. *Sede Vacante*

THIRD SUNDAY OF LENT

MARCH 3, 2013

In the transition between popes, the Catholic Church experiences **99**
a kind of odd suspension of her ordinary life. Of course, it is the
Spirit, not the pope, who animates the church. Still, there is some-
thing jarring when, during the eucharistic prayer, the ordinary
prayer for the pope by name is skipped over. It is also catnip for
churchy people, fostering anxiously giddy speculation about who
the next pope will be. The convergence of this period with further
revelations of sexual misconduct by Catholic clerics prompted my
reflections on what we might want from a pope, while recognizing
that, as any decent pope will tell you, our hope is rooted not in
popes, but in God.

READINGS: Exodus 3:1–8a, 13–15;
1 Corinthians 10:1–6, 10–12; Luke 13:1–9

It has been an interesting week to be a Catholic.
Of course everybody who has access to any form of media
knows that Pope Benedict's resignation from the papacy
took effect on Thursday
and that the church has entered
a period of *sede vacante*,
when the chair of Peter is empty

as we await the election of a new pope
by the college of cardinals.

In my mind, this event is framed
by two other events from this week:
On Monday the Scottish Cardinal Keith O'Brien
resigned amid accusations
of sexual misconduct with several priests,
and on Friday the Archdiocese of Baltimore
issued a statement that one of my brother deacons
had been suspended from ministry
after his arrest for possession of child pornography.

Sad to say, for all too many people
such news has ceased to be shocking,
because it has come to seem
like business as usual
from the Catholic Church.
And I find myself praying
that God will seize this opportunity
to send us a leader who can make the church
into the kind of place where such things
at least regain their capacity to shock.

So what does the word of God offer us today?
We hear in the Gospel the parable of the fig tree,
which for three years produces no fruit,
after which the owner of the orchard,
justly and understandably frustrated,
tells the gardener to cut it down
so that it will no longer deplete the soil.
But the gardener pleads with the owner

to give the tree one more year,
during which he will tend it and fertilize it.

Early Christian interpreters such as Saint Augustine
saw the parable as a warning to Christians that,
while we have been granted another season of grace
in which to bear the fruit of good works,
a day of judgment and reckoning is coming
for those whose lives remain barren.

But perhaps this parable
is not just about us as individuals,
but also about us as a church.
Events not just this week
but over the past ten years
have led me often to wonder
whether our church
has become like the fig tree,
exhausting the soil around it
while producing no fruit
but scandal upon scandal,
sucking life from the world
and offering nothing in return
but one more excuse
for the cynicism
that so pervades modern life.
Is time running out
for our church to bear good fruit?
Could the day arrive when God decides
that the time has come to cut it down?
Christ said that the gates of hell
would not prevail against his church,

but we must also remember
the words of Saint Paul:
"Whoever thinks he is standing secure
should take care not to fall."

These are dark thoughts to have
on the eve of a papal election.
And they bring with them
the temptation to think
that what is needed to fix the church

is a pope who fits with my particular agenda—
whether that is a pope who will
ordain women to the priesthood
or impose the Latin Mass on all parishes,
or change the church's teaching on contraception
or excommunicate all the bad Catholics.
These might be good ideas or bad ideas,
but a solution more radical
than any of these is called for—
a solution that fits
neither a "conservative" agenda
nor a "liberal" one,
a solution that is hinted at
in the parable of the fig tree.

The gardener in the parable says
that he will cultivate the ground
around the tree and fertilize it.
What our translation
rather primly translates as "fertilizer"
is the Greek word *kopria*,
which really means "excrement."
A pope from many centuries ago, Gregory the Great,

said in reference to this parable
that the fertilizer that can make
the unfruitful tree of our souls fruitful once again
is the remembrance of the dung of our past sins;
the frank acknowledgement
of the stench of our own misdeeds
can pierce our hearts
and move us to begin bearing
the fruit of good and godly deeds (Homily 31).

And what is true of us as individuals
is just as true of us as a church.
The church must clear away
all of the weeds that are choking it:
the desire to protect careers and images at all costs,
the denial that the world's evils
are found in the church as well,
the denigration of any who would
dare to call us to account.
The church must be fertilized by facing up
to the foulness of her failings,
and letting her heart be pierced
by the stench of her own sins,
so that we can in due season bear fruit
that will feed a world that is spiritually starving.

Perhaps our next pope can help us to do this.
But the church stands
on the promise of Christ to remain with us,
not on the dream of a pope
who will fix everything that is wrong with us.
Still, we should pray in this time of *sede vacante*
for God to send us a leader

who, like the gardener in the parable,
will cultivate and fertilize the church
with honest repentance.
And we should not only pray
but pray with confidence,
because we know that while our past is ours,
and we must own it,
our future belongs to the God
whose grace can make a barren fig tree fruitful
and make a desert bush burn

with the fire of God's presence,
the God whose Spirit,
despite our best efforts to quench it,
still burns as a refiner's fire within the church,
the living body of Christ.

17. *Nasara*

TWENTIETH SUNDAY IN ORDINARY TIME

AUGUST 17, 2014

The deadly attacks by the Islamic State (ISIS) on religious mi-
norities and Pope Francis's call for prayer for persecuted Christians
coincided with the lectionary presenting us with the somewhat
shocking story of Jesus's initial refusal to heal the daughter of the
Canaanite woman. A call to prayer for persecuted Christians is
something to be lauded and heeded, but it can be twisted into
a parochial concern for the members of our "team," a way of
highlighting the suffering of our "side" as somehow unique. The
exchange between Jesus and the woman calls into question the
whole notion of teams and sides, at least as regards God's concern
for those who suffer, and ought to make us think differently about
how we pray.

READINGS: Isaiah 56:1, 6–7; Romans 11:13–15, 29–32;
Matthew 15:21–28

In today's Gospel we hear the surprising exchange
between Jesus and the Canaanite woman
who asks him to heal her daughter.
What surprises us is Jesus's
seeming reluctance to help the woman
because she is not among

the "lost sheep of the house of Israel."
At first he ignores her request,
and then he compares her to a dog
who is not worthy to eat the bread
of the children of Israel.
The woman does not blink at this insult,
but cleverly turns the tables,
saying that even dogs
get to eat the scraps that fall to the floor.
Jesus then changes his tune—

saying, "O woman, great is your faith!"—
and heals her daughter.

Early Christian and medieval interpreters of this story
generally thought that Jesus
intended to help the woman all along,
but initially resisted her request
so that she could show to his disciples
the depth of the faith she possessed.
Writing in the fourth century,
Saint John Chrysostom said,
"Jesus did not want the great virtue in this woman
to be hidden.
He did not speak these words to insult her,
but to call her forth,
and to reveal the treasure contained in her"
(*Homilies on Matthew* 52).
It may come as no surprise to some of you
that I think that the early Christian
and medieval interpreters
are on to something in at least this regard:
Matthew does not offer this story
as a learning moment for Jesus

but as a learning moment
for his disciples and for us.

The disciples learn through this exchange
that even though Jesus has indeed been sent
"to the lost sheep of the house of Israel,"
God's gift and call to faith are not restricted
to any one people, any one group.
Even those whom they considered outsiders
could possess great faith—
faith, indeed, greater than their own.
Isaiah prophesied that the foreigners
who love and serve the Lord
would be brought by God to the holy mount Zion,
to offer prayer and sacrifice in God's temple,
which "will be called a house of prayer for all peoples."
Jesus initially stresses the woman's outsider status
only to make more striking
the praise he lavishes on her faith,
as if to say that the time
of universal reconciliation
foretold by Isaiah
was now arriving in the healing power
available to all through Jesus.

Jesus's exchange with the woman also teaches us
who are his disciples today
that we are to be a community
in which racial, ethnic,
and other human divisions
are overcome and reconciled.
The church is,
as the Second Vatican Council taught,

to be a sacrament—a sign and cause—
of the unity of the human race;
it should be a house of prayer for all peoples.
The nations should be able to look at us and see
what a world reconciled and restored to God looks like.

We do not, unfortunately, need any help to see
what an *un*reconciled, *un*restored world looks like.
We see the attacks on religious minorities in Iraq
by the forces of the so-called

Islamic State of Iraq and Syria or ISIS.
We see the other places
that have been in the news this week,
in which religious, ethnic, and racial differences
have led to violence:
between Israeli and Palestinian in Gaza,
between Black and white in Ferguson, Missouri.
And then there are the places
that may have slipped from our sight in recent days:
Afghanistan, Egypt, Central America,
Syria, Nigeria, Sudan, Ukraine.
We have seen what occurs
when one group of people looks at another
and says, "You are dogs,
unworthy of God's love and healing,"
and are blind to the possibility of great faith
in those who are other,
those who are different.
In the midst of this violence, we
as individuals and as a community
have been entrusted by Christ
with the ministry of reconciliation.

But what can we do
in the midst of such conflict and division?
How do we begin to exercise
our ministry of reconciliation—
we who ourselves so often think
in terms of "us" and "them,"
we who ourselves often need
so desperately to be reconciled?
Perhaps at least a first step
would be to invite into our hearts through prayer
all those situations of conflict, hatred, and division,
asking God's peace to descend
not only on those we see
as innocent victims
but also on those we see
as the sources of conflict and hatred.

Pope Francis has asked that we pray today
for Christians in Iraq
who have been driven from their homes
and in some cases killed.
As many of you have undoubtedly seen in news reports,
the homes of Christians in northern Iraq
have been marked by the ISIS militants
with the Arabic letter *nūn*,
which stands for *Nasara*,
which is the term in the Qur'an for Christians,
the followers of Jesus of Nazareth.
These Christians have been faced
with the choice of converting to Islam
or abandoning their homes and belongings
and fleeing their cities.

Most have chosen to cling to their faith
and abandon everything else.
These people need our prayers,
as do the other persecuted religious minorities in Iraq
who have also been forced to flee their homes,
and face starvation and death.
But for the true seeds of reconciliation
to take root in our hearts,
we must also pray
for the enemies of our fellow Christians in Iraq:

those who seem to have no interest in reconciliation,
those who have committed acts of unspeakable brutality,
those who are most in need of the peace of Christ.
Our hearts must become houses of prayer for all peoples.

But this kind of prayer is hard;
to respond with love in the face of insult and injury
requires faith as great as that of the Canaanite woman.
But it is such faith, such prayer,
that will, by God's grace,
truly mark us as *Nasara*:
followers of Jesus of Nazareth.

18. Family

There is probably nothing that is more intramural than a church **111**
synod. A papal conclave and election is, with all its arcane proce-
dures, something of an object of fascination for those outside the
church, but a synod is pretty boring stuff for those not invested
in the particular issue. The 2015 synod on the family, however,
touched on sexuality, divorce, and other issues. These are not only
of fairly intense interest to people in the church, but they also
attract outside attention since Catholic teaching on these matters
is so kinkily out of step with modern Western sensibilities that
they elicit a kind of prurient interest in Catholic discussions. The
convergence of this event in the life of the church with Mark's
presentation of Jesus's strict teaching on divorce and marriage
prompted these reflections on families and how we can be faith-
ful to the gospel's demands while holding fast to trust in God's
merciful love.

READINGS: Genesis 2:18–24; Hebrews 2:9–11; Mark 10:2–16

As some of you may know, today in Rome
there begins the second phase
of the Synod on the Family.
A synod is a meeting of bishops and others
from around the world

to deliberate on matters of importance to the church:
in this case, 279 bishops from 120 countries.
The *Instrumentum laboris*, or "working paper,"
that lays out an agenda for the synod
gives some idea of the topics that will be discussed:
divorce, annulments,
domestic violence, work pressures,
the plight of migrant and refugee families,
contraception, same-sex marriages, poverty,
as well as how the faith is or is not

passed on within families.

Call me pessimistic, but I suspect
that three weeks might not be enough time
to find adequate ways
to address all of these issues.
But given the changes and challenges
to family life in the world today
it's at least a start.

During the first phase of the synod last year,
one of the most controversial—
and still unsettled—issues
was the pastoral care of those
who are divorced and remarried,
particularly the question of participation
in the sacramental life of the church.
And our Gospel reading this morning
puts us smack dab
in the middle of that controversy.
Here we seem to find Jesus
at his most uncompromising:
"What God has joined together,
no human being must separate. . . .

Whoever divorces his wife and marries another
commits adultery against her;
and if she divorces her husband
and marries another,
she commits adultery."
The judgment passed in these words
strikes our ears harshly;
these words seem lacking in mercy,
lacking in appreciation
for life's complexity and difficulty,
particularly in the emotionally fraught area
of the family.

But do we really want to accuse Jesus
of not appreciating
life's complexity and difficulty,
he who was made perfect through suffering?
Do we really want to say
that Jesus does not understand
that real-life families do not fit easily
into an idealized model,
that he does not know that, to be honest,
it is not just marriages that end in divorce
that are "broken,"
but that all families come
with some level
of brokenness
or dysfunction
or just plain weirdness?

He knows this.
Of course he knows this.
Jesus's own family was, shall we say,
decidedly "nontraditional";

and in not being ashamed,
as our second reading says,
to be called our brother
he has proudly joined himself
to our real-life families
in all their brokenness
and dysfunction
and weirdness.

What then of this uncompromising teaching
on divorce and remarriage?
Let us take Jesus at his word.
Let us presume he really means
that marriage creates an unbreakable bond,
such that it really is impossible
to forge a new bond to replace the old.
Let us further presume that he really thinks
that with the coming of God's kingdom
it is now possible, through God's grace,
for his followers to overcome
the hard-heartedness
that has so often torn apart
the two whom God had made one flesh.

I do not know how all of this
fits together with God's mercy—
some things remain mysteries to us in this life—
but I do know that even if we grant all this,
we still have no reason to think
that Jesus means for his words to be used as a stick
to beat up on those who do not live up to them.
We have no reason to think
that Jesus does not continue to love
those whose families break up

or break down
or break apart.
We have no reason to think
that Jesus ever abandons us,
no matter how broken
or dysfunctional
or just plain weird
our family lives might be.
The bishops must listen to the words of Jesus,
but I pray they will hear them as the words of one
who has plunged headlong
into all the complexity and ambiguity
of human love,
of human longing,
of human solace and sorrow.
It is only then that they will hear them truly.

Speaking last week in Philadelphia,
Pope Francis said,
"In families, there is always, always, the cross.
Always. . . .
But, in families as well, after the cross,
there is the resurrection.
Because the Son of God opened for us this path."
As followers of Jesus,
all of us are trying to walk that path
through the cross to the resurrection.
Indeed, we are called to find the resurrection
within our broken,
dysfunctional,
weird families—
not beyond them—
because it is precisely in real families,
not ideal families,

that we learn what it means
to have faith,
to have hope,
to have love.

That's the funny thing about families:
They don't have to be perfect
in order for God's grace to work through them.
We all fail to some degree
as spouses and parents,
as children and siblings.
But in the midst of our failure
a miracle can occur.
With the help of God's grace,
we can manage to love each other,
even as we struggle to show that love,
to accept that love,
to bear the burden of that love.

There are no perfect families;
but only families where love might grow
like a stubborn weed
that no amount of
human brokenness
or dysfunction
or weirdness
can uproot.
Sometimes we must carry our love
like a cross,
but in faith we carry it with Jesus
on the path of resurrection.

19. Manna Gathering

EIGHTEENTH SUNDAY IN ORDINARY TIME

AUGUST 4, 2018

Every summer for a decade and a half I have joined others who study the history of Christian theology at the Boston Colloquy in Historical Theology for several days of rigorous and collegial discussion. Though sponsored by a Catholic university, it is not an exclusively Catholic gathering; it draws scholars from a variety of Christian traditions, as well as the occasional nonbeliever. It is a place where the relevance of the past for the present, including the present-day life of the church, is taken seriously. A Mass is always offered toward the end of the program for Catholics and others who may wish to come. The congregation is pretty unusual. Almost everyone present has a PhD in theology and a body of uniquely obscure knowledge, along with strong opinions about the tradition of the church. In other words, it's a tough audience. The privilege of preaching at the 2018 meeting gave me an opportunity to reflect on the intersection of ecclesial faith and academic scholarship, and our relation as Christians to the past.

READINGS: Exodus 16:2–4, 12–15; Ephesians 4:17, 20–24;
John 6:24–35

I am put in mind of our vocation
as historical theologians

when I hear of the Hebrews
in today's first reading
given miraculous bread by the Lord
to sustain them on their desert journey,
bread that appeared each morning
for them to gather before it vanished,
bread that is identified in today's Gospel
as a foreshadowing of Jesus Christ,
God's incarnate Word,
the true bread come down from heaven.
"On seeing it, the Israelites
asked one another, 'What is this?'
for they did not know what it was.
But Moses told them,
'This is the bread that the Lord
has given you to eat.'"

The Word of God
has been spread abroad in human history.
It lies before us like miraculous bread,
the food of the kingdom
upon which we will feast eternally,
waiting to be gathered
so that it may nourish us
on our pilgrimage through that history
to the new Jerusalem.
We gather what has been spread abroad,
the supersubstantial bread of the Word,
finding it sometimes in the most unlikely places:
Christologies of mixture and early Christian dialogues,
the writings of James of Eltville and of Reginald Pole,
texts from Saint Thomas and, yes, even Duns Scotus.
We come across a previously unknown manuscript

or some long-ignored passage in Augustine
and we ask one another, "What is this?"
It is the bread that the Lord has given us to eat,
and not just us, but all of God's pilgrim people.

As we ply our craft, in archives and classrooms,
committee meetings and academic colloquies,
we should always bear in our hearts those words:
It is the bread that the Lord has given you to eat.
And even more we should bear in our hearts
the words of Jesus:
"Do not work for food that perishes
but for the food that endures for eternal life,
which the Son of Man will give you. . . .
I am the bread of life;
whoever comes to me will never hunger,
and whoever believes in me will never thirst."

The bishop Theophylact
wrote in the eleventh century,
"He is the bread not of this ordinary life,
but of a very different kind of life,
which death will never cut short."
But the true mystery of the Word made flesh
is that the bread of extraordinary life
is given to us mortals in this ordinary life,
the ordinary time of human history.
We seek out the bread of deathless life
amid the ambiguities of the past,
the power-plays and human failings,
the stumbling efforts at human holiness
and the sanctified stubbornness of saints.
The task of the historical theologian as theologian

is to gather the manna scattered
on the shifting sands of time,
which do not provide
the comforting stability of abstraction.
We seek the bread of life
that death will never cut short
in a confrontation with thinkers
possessed of mentalities
very different from our own,
but with the confidence that because
they too hungered
for food that never perishes,
and they too thirsted
for the living water,
it is not impossible that we can hear
echoed in their words
the one Word of life.

The chasm imposed by historical distance
cannot separate us from these friends,
not because we have honed
our skills of historical imagination
(though I hope we have done that),
and not because we have labored
to acquire facility with dead languages
(though I hope we have done that),
and not because of we have toiled
to gain paleographical skills
(though I hope people other than me
have done that),
but because we, like they,
have been given to eat of the bread of life.
They, like us, have hungered and thirsted,

and they, like us, have been fed by Christ
with the bread of angels
so that the one Word
might sound in their words.
We gather their words with care,
for it is the bread that the Lord
has given us to eat.

20. Grand Jury

122   *When the Pennsylvania grand jury report on sexual abuse and its cover-up in the Catholic Church was released on August 14, 2018, I knew on an intellectual level that it contained little that was new. Many of the crimes it documented had occurred years and decades earlier. Also, the report did little to acknowledge the remedial steps the church had taken over the course of those decades. But following closely on the heels of revelations of abuse by Theodore McCarrick, the (now-defrocked) cardinal archbishop of Washington, the sheer volume of cases documented by the grand jury report, and the grim details it contained, swept aside any caveats one might have wanted to offer about how things had changed. Whatever the current state of affairs in the church—and despite some progress there remains much work still to do, particularly with regard to holding leaders responsible—the past has to be reckoned with. This homily was my small contribution to that reckoning.*

READINGS: Joshua 24:1–2a, 15–17, 18b;
Ephesians 5:2a, 25–32; John 6:60–69

Today's readings seem almost tailor-made
for this moment in the church's life.

In the Gospel, many of those hearing Jesus's words
are offended and walk away:
"Many of his disciples
returned to their former way of life
and no longer accompanied him."
In Paul's Letter to the Ephesians
we hear of Christ's love for the church
"cleansing her by the bath of water with the word . . .
that she might be holy and without blemish."
In our first reading, Joshua challenges the Israelites:
"Decide today whom you will serve,"
and we hear them reaffirm their commitment to God:
"Far be it from us to forsake the Lord
for the service of other gods."
It might seem that the obvious message today would be
an exhortation to stay committed to the church,
to not walk away and return to your former way of life,
to not lose hope in the face of past and present scandals
but to trust in God's power to cleanse
and purify the church
which despite all the sin and betrayal
remains Christ's beloved bride.

That would be a pretty good homily.
In fact, that was more or less
the homily I preached two weeks ago.
And I would stand by all of what I said then,
even in light of the tidal wave of evidence
of misdeeds by priests and bishops
that crashed over the church last week
with the release of the Pennsylvania grand jury report.
I still feel that I must say
with the apostles in today's Gospel

"Master, to whom shall we go?
You have the words of eternal life."

But I don't think that this
is what the Spirit is saying to the Church
in today's Scriptures.
I believe that today the Spirit
is exhorting all of us to speak truthfully.
Because in today's Scriptures
it is not any misdeed that offends people,
it is not any scandal or sin that sends them away,
but it is the life-giving words of Jesus—
words that are Spirit and life—
at which they take offense.
It is one thing to be scandalized
by Jesus's words of Spirit and life
and choose to remain
in your untransformed way of life;
it is something else to be scandalized
by the sins of those who claim
to speak in Jesus's name
and choose to follow another path.
On the whole, I would say that people today
are not walking away from the church
because they are offended by Jesus's words.
That would be refreshing.
I think they leave because they have come
asking for the bread of life
and have been given a stone or a snake instead.
They come looking for the life-changing challenge
of being a disciple of the crucified and risen Jesus
and are all too often told to just sit there quietly
and not make too much noise.

They come looking for the community of the Spirit
and find an institution more concerned
with saving face than saving souls.

Our leaders bear much responsibility for this.
They bear responsibility because of the unspeakable acts
committed by a relatively small percentage of the clergy,
often against the weakest and most vulnerable
of Christ's little ones.
They bear responsibility because of the cover-ups
perpetrated by a relatively large percentage of bishops,
who thought that the souls of these little ones
were worth sacrificing
for the sake of the church's reputation.
They bear responsibility because they too often
have heard Jesus's words of Spirit and life
and turned back to worship the gods of this world,
gods of pleasure and wealth and pretense,
gods who thrive on secrecy and lies.

Our leaders bear much responsibility.
But, in a different sense, we too bear a responsibility.
If we want a church
that welcomes people
into the adventure of discipleship,
that values truth over reputation,
that speaks words of Spirit and life,
then those words must come from *our* mouths.
This is the burden of our prophetic call
that we received at our baptisms.

I think of the victims of clerical abuse
and of their families,

who, when the powerful in the church
told them to just sit there quietly,
raised their voices in divine outrage
and bore the cross of rejection and dismissal.
They bore that burden in the hope
that speaking words of truth,
words of Spirit and life,
is more healing than suffering silence
and more powerful than face-saving lies.
They bore that burden

not only for themselves
but for all of us,
because only words of Spirit and life
can save us now.

But they should no longer bear that burden alone.
Let us take upon our own shoulders
the burden of truthful speaking,
by acknowledging the failings of the church,
by working for a church that can hear the truth,
by hoping for a church that can truly be
"the church in splendor,
without spot or wrinkle or any such thing . . .
holy and without blemish."
Let us speak Jesus's words of Spirit and life,
and let those who reject those words
turn away to serve other gods.

21. Saint Oscar Romero

The canonization of a saint in the Catholic Church is one of those   **127**
aspects of church life that holds a certain fascination for both
Catholics and non-Catholics. The arcane multistage process, the
role of miracles in the determination of sanctity, even the notion
of holiness itself, all highlight some of the more exotic elements of
Catholicism. The specific case of Archbishop Oscar Romero (1917–
1980) points to the complex intersection of church and world, since
there was controversy within the church over whether Romero
had died as a martyr for the faith or as a political activist. At one
point his canonization process was stalled for a number of years
due to the controversial nature of his ministry and witness. After
a year of multiple examples of pastoral malpractice by prelates, his
canonization in 2018 provided a moment of relief at being able
to point to a bishop whose life and death proclaimed the gospel of
Christ so unambiguously.

READINGS: Wisdom 7:7–11; Hebrews 4:12–13;
    Mark 10:17–30

If Jesus's words in today's Gospel
do not make most of us profoundly uncomfortable
then we are not really paying attention.

"It is easier for a camel to pass through the eye of a needle
than for one who is rich to enter the kingdom of God."
Maybe we are not paying attention
to the words themselves
or maybe we are not paying attention to our own lives.
Even with our genuine struggles
trying to pay tuitions or credit card debt
or mortgages or medical bills,
we citizens of the modern developed world
still live in a material abundance

that surpasses the richest person of Jesus's day
and most people alive in our own day.
"How hard it is for those who have wealth
to enter the kingdom of God."
As the Letter to the Hebrews says,
"the word of God . . . is sharper
than any two-edged sword . . .
everything is naked and exposed to the eyes
of him to whom we must render an account."
If we are not squirming,
if we are not feeling God's word
penetrating to the deepest thoughts of our hearts,
then we are just not paying attention.

But Jesus is not, I think, simply trying
to make us feel guilty—
though exploiting the motivating power of guilt
is a fine Catholic tradition that I, as a parent, approve of.
Nor is he saying that our prosperity
is somehow in itself evil.
Jesus's concern for the rich man who asks him,
"what must I do to inherit eternal life?"
is not simply that he make himself poor.

The key to understanding Jesus's words
to the rich man is not
"Go, sell what you have, and give to the poor"
but what is next: "Then come, follow me."
Like Solomon in our first reading,
Jesus calls the rich man to give up what he has
in order to gain something far more valuable,
the heavenly treasure of wisdom.
Jesus, divine wisdom made flesh,
calls him to give up
everything that holds him back
from being his disciple,
everything that holds him back
from following in the way of wisdom,
which is Jesus's way of cross and resurrection.
The act of giving his wealth to the poor
is simply the prelude to following Jesus.

It is true that it is often our material possessions
that hold us back,
the things that we accumulate
and on which we stake our happiness,
which form walls around us
to protect us from God and from other people.
But those protective walls
can be built of other, less tangible, things as well:
our self-images,
our reputations,
our ideologies,
our compulsions and our addictions.
These are all burdens that Jesus calls us to give up
in order to be free to follow him on
the path of discipleship.

But can we answer this call?
Can we become free enough to follow Jesus's way?
We are, after all, just ordinary people.

Today in Rome, in the solemn rite of canonization,
the church declared to be a saint
Archbishop Oscar Romero of San Salvador,
who was killed by a government death squad
while celebrating Mass on March 24, 1980.
When he became bishop of San Salvador in 1977
Romero was seen
by both the government and the church
as an ordinary bishop, a "safe" bishop,
one who was traditional in his theology
and unwilling to interfere in politics—
one who would not cause trouble.
But when priests who worked among the poor
and advocated for their rights
began turning up dead,
killed by government-sponsored death squads,
Romero's eyes were opened
to the plight of the poor in his country,
and he began speaking out
against government repression.
The day before he was killed,
he made a direct appeal
to the soldiers in the military:
"No soldier is obliged to obey
an order contrary to the law of God.
No one has to obey an immoral law.
It is high time you recovered your consciences
and obeyed your consciences
rather than a sinful order. . . .

In the name of God,
in the name of this suffering people
whose cries rise to heaven
more loudly each day,
I implore you,
I beg you,
I order you in the name of God:
Stop the repression."

Like the rich man in today's Gospel,
Oscar Romero heard the call of Jesus
to give up everything—
the favor of church and state,
his previous ideas of what it meant to be a bishop,
and ultimately even his life—
in order to learn true wisdom
by following Jesus on the way of the cross.
His example pleads with us,
just as he pleaded with the soldiers of El Salvador,
to value the wisdom of God above all else,
to let the two-edged sword of God's word
probe our consciences,
to listen to the voice of God
and be willing to surrender everything
for the sake of God.

Oscar Romero was an ordinary man,
someone who, like us,
lived behind protective walls
of money and power,
of ideology and self-image,
of reputation and prestige.
But Jesus called him forth from that ordinary life

and stripped him of every worldly protection
and placed him amid
the demonic powers of hatred and greed
with nothing except the love of God to clothe him,
nothing but the cross of Christ to shelter him.
God made this ordinary man a saint
by teaching him the wisdom of the cross.
And God will make us saints as well,
if we are willing to practice the daily discipline
of paying attention to Jesus's call

to come follow him,
of paying attention to our lives
and all that holds us back
from answering that call,
to open ourselves to the grace
that can transform the ordinary
into the extraordinary.
Saint Oscar Romero,
pray for us.

PART 4

Feasts and Festivals

A specific subset of events in the life of the church are the celebrations tied to the liturgical year. Some of these celebrations, particularly Christmas and Easter, bring large crowds, many of whom are not particularly frequent or regular churchgoers. This demographic fact is an opportunity, but it should not dominate the celebration. Some preachers (though, in my experience, fewer than anecdotes might lead you to believe) use this opportunity to scold the slackers. Others try to offer an upbeat message that ends up hollow, inane, and boring (it's important to remember that infrequent attenders are not necessarily spiritually unserious). Still others, overwhelmed by the occasion, try to say everything a seeker might need to know and end up communicating little.

Even apart from the question of who is listening, these events, because they often come with a set of expectations and tend to have the same readings year after year, pose a particular homiletic challenge: What new can (or should) be found to say? One can be so tempted by the desire to be novel that one ends up saying something foolish or beside the point. On the other hand, one can simply give up, recycle old sermons, and ignore the way in which the liturgical flow of time intersects and interrupts the flow of worldly time. In this sense, each festival is unique: The Easter three months after my mother died (homily 24) is different from the Easter that came days after the burning of the Cathedral of Notre Dame (homily 28), and both of these are different from the Easter celebrated in the midst of a global pandemic (homily 31).

The encounter of the unchanging rhythms of the lectionary and liturgical calendar with the unexpected and often chaotic events of daily life creates the syncopation of Christian existence. It is an existence in which what Augustine called "the storms of incoherent events [that] tear to pieces my thoughts" can find a kind of redemption by being placed within the narrative of God's redeeming love. It seems to me that it is one of the privileges of preaching on the great festivals of the church to be able to bring together the key moments of that narrative with the ongoing story of the world.

22. Mary and the Fire-Folk

The Solemnity of the Assumption of the Blessed Virgin Mary is a **135** *peculiarly Roman Catholic feast, and one that might be thought of as a kind of "extension" of the biblical stories of Mary, particularly of her statement in the Magnificat that God has "exalted those who are lowly." Not unlike the Ascension of Christ, the Assumption of Mary is clothed in imagery of an outdated cosmology (see homily 25), and in this way can pose a challenge for those who in most areas of life have abandoned that cosmology. So this homily attempts to make sense of this feast for those whose minds are shaped by modern notions of the cosmos, by pointing to Mary's Assumption as a sign of our own eschatological hopes.*

READINGS: Revelation 11:19a; 12:1–6a, 10ab;
1 Corinthians 15:20–27; Luke 1:39–56

Although we habitually speak
of heaven as "up" and of hell as "down,"
I suspect that most of us know,
as most Christians have always known,
that neither place can be reached
by traversing a physical distance.
Indeed, a number of years ago

Pope John Paul II reiterated
the traditional Christian view,
saying, "The 'heaven' or 'happiness'
in which we will find ourselves
is neither an abstraction
nor a physical place in the clouds,
but a living, personal relationship with the Holy Trinity"
(General Audience, Wednesday, July 21, 1999).
In other words, "heaven" is not so much a place
as it is a state of being.

It is good to remind ourselves of this
when we celebrate a feast
such as the one we celebrate today.
Today, the Feast of the Assumption,
we celebrate our belief
that Mary, upon her death,
was taken body and soul into heavenly glory.
Already in AD 451, when the Emperor Marcian
asked the bishop of Jerusalem
to bring Mary's bones to Constantinople
so that they might be placed in the cathedral there,
the bishop responded to his request by saying that
"Mary had died in the presence of the apostles;
but her tomb, when opened later . . .
was found empty
and so the apostles concluded
that the body was taken up into heaven."
Universal acceptance of this belief
developed over the centuries in the Church
until it was solemnly defined
by Pope Pius XII in 1950
as part of the official body of teachings
of the Catholic Church.

Now one might imagine this event
as one often sees it depicted in art,
with Mary slowly rising up into the clouds,
perhaps with angels beneath her feet
giving her an extra boost.
But if heaven is not a physical place,
but rather a state of being
in perfect relationship with God—
a state that involves a radical transformation
of our entire self, body and soul—
then these artistic imaginings
must be understood as precisely that:
acts of the human imagination
in which we attempt to depict for ourselves
realities that go beyond what our minds can fully grasp.
So when we speak of Mary
being "assumed" or taken up into heaven,
we aren't really talking about a direction
to which we can point
or a distance that we can traverse.
Mary is not, literally speaking, "up there"
because heaven is not, literally speaking, "up there."

But it is not too hard to imagine
why people have spoken that way over the years.
There is something about the sky—
or as we sometimes call them, the heavens—
that speaks to us of that exalted state of being
that we might call "heavenly glory,"
that state of being into which Mary has entered.

This summer,
while on vacation in northwestern Colorado,
in one of those increasingly rare places

where there is no electrical lighting for miles around,
I was amazed by the night sky.
In contrast to Baltimore, where at night our stingy skies
might favor us with at best a glimpse of the Big Dipper,
there the stars were strewn across the sky
with reckless prodigality.
Their number and their variety
were almost more
than the mind and senses could take in.
The immensity of the space of the sky

was like a pool into which one could fall forever.
I was put in mind of the words
of the Jesuit poet Gerard Manley Hopkins:
"Look at the stars! Look, look up at the skies!
 O look at all the fire-folk sitting in the air!"
It was as if in the sky above us
God had provided the whole world
with a symbol of heavenly glory.
The night sky spoke of a mystery
in which there is always more to discover,
a pearl of great price
for which it just might make sense
to risk everything,
a standing invitation
to join the fire-folk dwelling there in glory.
It made it possible to imagine
that what spread itself out above me
was not merely a sky,
but was indeed the heavens.

What better place to imagine Mary,
"a woman clothed with the sun,
with the moon under her feet,

and on her head a crown of twelve stars"?
Surely of all Christ's followers,
Mary is among the fire-folk,
those in whom God's grace
has kindled the fire of divine love.
Saint Augustine wrote,
"My weight is my love.
Wherever I am carried, my love is carrying me.
By your gift we are set on fire and carried upwards;
we grow red hot and ascend" (*Confessions* 13.9.10).
Mary loved God,
and that love has carried her
into heavenly glory.

It is perhaps fitting that,
on this feast of Mary's being taken up
into the mystery that we call heaven,
our Gospel lets Mary herself speak
of the love that burns within her,
the divine gift by which
she is carried upward.
She sings in her Magnificat—
her song of praise to God—
of the love that casts down
the mighty from their thrones
and has lifted up the lowly.
Mary is lifted up in her lowliness
because she said yes to God's love,
said yes to the invitation
to become the mother of Jesus, God with us.

But this feast is not just about Mary,
for Mary is not only the Mother of God

but also the first disciple,
the first to say yes to Jesus Christ.
And all of us who say yes to Jesus
stand with Mary.
We have hope
that Mary's destiny in heavenly glory
will also be our destiny;
we have hope
that the unimaginable joy
of eternal life with God
will be ours as well;
we have hope
that we too will be among the fire-folk
who burn with divine love.

So heaven may not be "up"
and hell may not be "down,"
but the next time you happen
to be away from the city's lights
and the night is particularly clear,
and you find yourself beneath
that great symbol of heaven,
"Look at the stars! Look, look up at the skies!
O look at all the fire-folk sitting in the air!"
Imagine Mary among the stars in glory,
and imagine yourself there too.

23. Scarcity and Abundance

CORPUS CHRISTI

JUNE 2, 2013

Sometimes a celebration of the liturgical calendar can be the oc- *casion to question something that we might ordinarily think to be unquestionable—in this case, the law of scarcity. The Solemnity of the Body and Blood of Christ (commonly called Corpus Christi) is another distinctively Roman Catholic feast, celebrated in the United States on the Sunday following Trinity Sunday. The day is often marked by processions in which the sacrament is placed in a highly ornate vessel called a monstrance and displayed for the adoration of the faithful. In this homily, world events juxtaposed with Luke's account of the feeding of the multitudes provided an occasion to remind ourselves that Christ's sacred body does not dwell in splendid isolation from the world's suffering, but offers itself as the source of abundance in the midst of scarcity.*

READINGS: Genesis 14:18–22; 1 Corinthians 11:23–26; Luke 9:11b–17

On Friday I read a report that,
due to a combination
of a mismanaged national economy
and externally imposed import restrictions,
the Catholic Church in Venezuela

is facing a shortage of bread and wine
for the celebration of Mass.
(The nation is also facing a toilet paper shortage,
but that's another matter.)
It reminded me of how much what we do
within the walls of the church
is connected to the world outside the church,
the network of economic and political relations
that shape our lives.
This shortage of bread and wine in Venezuela
is an example of what people sometimes refer to
as the "law of scarcity."
The basic idea is that the less of something there is
the more its value increases.
If supply goes down and demand remains steady,
value—or at least the price—goes up.
The presumptions of the law of scarcity
are so woven into the fabric of our daily lives
that they come to seem unquestionable to us.
Of course something that is rare
is more valuable
than something that is abundant;
of course we are in competition,
even conflict,
with each other
for these valuable, limited goods.
It seems unquestionable.

In our reading today from Luke's Gospel, however,
we are invited to question this law of scarcity.
The story of the feeding of the multitudes begins
    in scarcity,
but rather than ending in conflict

and competition for those scarce goods,
it ends in an abundant feast for all who are there:
"They all ate and were satisfied."
In fact, more was left over than they began with.

In addition to being a sign
of the divine power incarnate in Jesus,
this story of the feeding of the multitudes
tells us something about the kingdom of God
 that Jesus comes to proclaim.
The economy of this kingdom
does not run according to the law of scarcity
but according to a law of abundance.
God provides us with more than enough
of God's love, God's mercy, God's grace.
And these things do not become any less valuable
on account of being supplied in abundance
or any less abundant
on account of being shared among many people.
Saint Augustine noted that
the citizens of earthly kingdoms
fight with each other for things that are in short supply:
glory, power, wealth, honor.
But in the case of divine goodness,
"anyone who refuses to share this possession
cannot have it;
and one who is most willing to let others share it in love
will have the greatest abundance" (*City of God* 15.5).

We should reflect on this story
of scarcity and abundance
in the context of our celebration
of the feast of Corpus Christi.

As in today's Gospel reading,
bread will be taken,
and blessed,
and broken,
and shared.
We will receive Christ's body and blood,
his soul and divinity,
under the sacramental signs
of bread and wine;
we will feed upon him spiritually,
and, as in today's Gospel,
we will be satisfied.
Indeed, not only will we be satisfied,
but the grace that is bestowed on us
is so abundant that there will be
twelve baskets left over—grace upon grace—
which we will take with us into a world
that is starving for both material food
and the food of God's mercy.

While the bread and wine shortages in Venezuela
show that the church is not removed
from the economic forces at work in the world,
in the end the Eucharist is not ruled
by the law of scarcity.
The value of the Eucharist is determined
not by what market forces do
to the price of bread and wine
but by what the Holy Spirit does with them,
transforming them into
the body and blood of God incarnate,
the food of immortality,
the cup of eternal salvation.

And the grace we receive in this sacrament
only increases as we leave this building
to share the love that we have received with others.

On this our feast of Corpus Christi,
it is right and just that we reflect
on the great gift of the body and blood of Christ
through which we as a community
have been abundantly blessed
for over a century and a quarter.
It is right and just to give thanks
for the thousands of Masses
that have been celebrated on our altars,
the bread of life that has been shared,
the hungry souls that have been satisfied.
It is right and just that we pause to adore
the God who bestows on us a gift so great
and in such abundance.
And it is right and just that we leave here
to share with others
the goodness that has filled our hearts.

24. Immortal Diamond

EASTER SUNDAY

MARCH 27, 2016

146   *The death of one's parent is both a universal human experience and something totally unique in every case, because every parent-child relationship is unique. Though I am not someone averse to using the first-person, either in writing or preaching, I also recognize the danger of putting oneself front and center when the focus of preaching is supposed to be the Triune God. Still, we all in some sense preach out of our own experience, and sometimes it works to do so explicitly. The death of my mother on January 30, 2016, coming as it did at the end of my extended visit to the Trappist monastery of Our Lady of Mepkin, near Charleston, South Carolina, prompted me to reflect on the nature of our existence in time and our hope for eternity, and Easter prompted me to put some of that reflection into words.*

READINGS: Acts 10:34a, 37–43; Colossians 3:1–4; John 20:1–9

Earlier this year
I spent several weeks at a Trappist monastery,
which is one of those things you can do
when you're a university professor on sabbatical
and your youngest child has left the nest for college.
Over the course of weeks I discovered

that not a lot happens at a Trappist monastery,
and every day is pretty much like the one before it
and the one after it.
You rise early at 3:00 a.m. and spend several hours
in communal and private prayer
before going off to work, praying some more,
then more work, and more prayers.
Throw in a few meals, eaten in silence,
and that's about your day.
The prayer itself is pretty much always the same:
chanting the 150 psalms over the course of two weeks,
along with a few hymns and Mass each day.
The work is also pretty much the same:
At this monastery it is growing mushrooms,
which is about as exciting as watching paint dry,
though more physically demanding.

Shortly before I left for the monastery
my mother was hospitalized.
She had been failing for several months
and it was clear to all of us
that the end was not too far off.
But my family insisted I not cancel my plans.
I arrived at the monastery knowing that I might well
have to cut short my time there,
as indeed proved to be the case
when my mother died three weeks later.

In the midst of those seemingly uneventful days,
prior to my mother's death,
I found myself thinking about
and praying over
the impermanence of life;
the way in which, despite our best efforts,

we cannot hold on to the things we love,
to the people we love;
how we hold our lives
like water cupped in our hands
that ever so slowly leaks through our fingers.
Our days slip past us,
each one marked by some degree of loss.
We experience this most sharply
when we lose to death someone we love.
We experience it perhaps less sharply,
but no less really,
as we drift away from friends over time
or lose the enthusiasm
we once felt for our work,
for a cause we cared about,
or even for our faith.

Of course, there are gains in life as well as losses,
but we experience a kind of loss even in life's gains.
As I prayed about the coming death of my mother
I recalled my last conversation with her,
in which she spoke of when I was a toddler
and she would come into my room every morning
and I would be standing in my crib,
so excited to see her.
While I have no doubt that she loved the man I became,
it was also clear that she missed that little toddler
and his unambiguous love and enthusiasm.
I thought too about my own children
and their transition from childhood
to young adulthood,
and how even in the process of becoming
the increasingly accomplished, interesting,
complex people that they are

there is the loss of innocent
childlike wonder and simplicity.
Even the great gains of life are not unmarked by loss.
The advent of the child who walks on her own
marks the end of the child
whom you carried in your arms.
The emergence of the child who can read for himself
marks the end of the child to whom you read
The Very Hungry Caterpillar
over and over and over and over.
As tired as our arms may grow,
and as tedious as the adventures
of that caterpillar may be,
we still miss the feel of that child against our chest,
the time spent together
discovering the wonder of language and image.
We want to hold on to those moments of grace,
but they pass away and even memory fades.

Is this simply the fate of us human beings,
who live within the unceasing stream of time?
Will the water of life inevitably
trickle through our fingers?
Does every tick of the clock
mark the winding down of life?
Is it the case, as the poet Gerard Manley Hopkins put it,
that "all is in an enormous dark/Drowned,"
that "vastness blurs and time beats level"?
Or can we find, in the midst of the ceaseless flow of time,
a still point, a place of eternity
in which every moment that flies past us
is held safe and kept close,
a point that gathers in all that time takes from us,
a point in which we can find that lost loved one,

that friendship that faded out over the years,
that childlike innocence
that was exchanged for adulthood?

On this Easter morning, Saint Paul exhorts us to
"think of what is above, not of what is on earth."
In the midst of this life that at every moment
is being pulled by time from our grasp,
Paul tells us to open our hands,
to let go of the things we love in this life.
But he tells us this not because this life is unimportant,
not because the things we love are not worthy of our love,
but because the only way we can keep them
is by releasing them
into the eternity of love that is God,
the eternity of love that explodes into our world
in the resurrection of Jesus.
This is what Easter hope is all about.
The empty tomb of Christ is the doorway
into the still point of eternity
in which all time is gathered and redeemed.
It is the doorway that we enter
through faith and baptism,
the faith that is expressed in the baptismal promises
that we will renew in a few moments.
And passing through that doorway, Saint Paul tells us,
we have died—
died to the merciless passage of time—
and our life is now hidden with Christ in God,
hidden in the risen one
who holds within himself all that we love.

What I found in the seemingly uneventful life
of prayer and work of the Trappist monks

was not a tedious cycle of pointless repetition
but the presence within time of eternity,
an eternity of returning again and again to the beginning,
to find that everything I thought time had taken
is being kept for me in the risen Jesus.
And it can be like this for all of us,
as we gather week by week
in the repetitive rhythm of the liturgy.
We return to our beginning,
we receive Jesus,
the eternal one,
into ourselves,
and find again in him
all that is true,
all that is good,
all that is beautiful.
We creatures of time,
who seem made for death,
whose best achievements
are shadowed by loss,
are given the gift of sharing in God's eternity
through Jesus Christ, who came to share our life
in the turbulent torrent of time,
so that we might share his life
in the still point of God's eternity.
To quote again the poet Hopkins:

> In a flash, at a trumpet crash,
> I am all at once what Christ is,
> since he was what I am, and
> This Jack, joke, poor potsherd, patch, matchwood,
> immortal diamond,
> Is immortal diamond.

25. Witness Protection

152 *The death of the radical priest Daniel Berrigan led me to focus, on this Ascension day, not so much on the mystery of Jesus's humanity being taken up into God, but on the meaning of the witness to which Jesus calls his disciples as he departs. Roman Catholics in the US are not notably evangelistic, though it is becoming increasingly apparent that the church can no longer depend on cultural and biological reproduction as a source of new members. Partly because Catholics often define themselves over and against forms of evangelicalism, "evangelism" can be a hard sell to Catholics. In this homily I hoped to suggest that, while Christian witness can take many forms, it is something that is integral to our faith. The particular witness of Dan Berrigan can expand our imaginations as to what evangelism might look like, but also reminds us of the boldness we have been called to through God's gift of the Holy Spirit.*

READINGS: Acts 1:1–11; Hebrews 9:24–28, 10:19–23;
Luke 24:46–53

Before he ascends into heaven,
Jesus recalls to his followers what they have seen—
his life, his death, his resurrection—

and says, "You are witnesses of these things."
"You are witnesses."
On the one hand, it is a statement
that they have been present
and have seen these wondrous things take place.
But it is also a call
not simply to *be* witnesses,
but also to *bear* witness.

To be a witness
you don't have to do anything
but be there and have your eyes open,
but to bear witness
you must be willing
to get on the stand
and give public testimony
to what you have seen.
The difference between being a witness
and bearing witness
becomes particularly clear in cases
of what we call "witness intimidation."
Often—all too often in our own city—
people might be witnesses to a crime
but are not willing to bear witness
because they fear for their safety
or the safety of their family,
because they do not believe
that the police can protect them from reprisal.

Jesus says to his disciples, however,
that no matter how intimidating it may be,
no matter what threats they may face,
because they have been witnesses

they must now bear witness.
Throughout his earthly ministry,
Jesus has been God's faithful witness,
speaking God's truth whatever the consequences,
showing God's love to the unlovable,
manifesting in his words and actions
the reality of God's kingdom.
At his ascension, Jesus bestows on his disciples
a share in this ministry of witness.
But he does not leave them

to do this on their own;
rather, he says to them,
"you will receive power
when the Holy Spirit comes upon you,
and you will be my witnesses in Jerusalem,
throughout Judea and Samaria,
and to the ends of the earth."
The Spirit will be given to them
so they can both *be* witnesses
and *bear* witness.

In the book of Acts,
the Holy Spirit gives the apostles
eyes to see the work of God
that is ongoing in their midst,
enabling them to discern the new reality
that the Spirit is creating.
It is the Spirit who enables them to see
that the gentiles, whom they had formerly viewed
as "outsiders" and "unclean,"
have now been brought
into the community of God's people
and made clean through the blood of Christ.

Likewise, it is the Spirit who enables them to see
that the power of imperial Rome,
which claims to dominate the known world,
is something they did not need to fear
and before which they do not need to bow,
because it is nothing compared to the power of God,
which has raised Jesus from the dead.
The Spirit gives them eyes to see
to be witnesses to God's work,
and the same Spirit empowers them to bear witness,
despite the "witness intimidation" that they face
from the religious and political authorities of their day.

We might say that the Spirit
is God's "witness protection program."
But, unlike what we see in the movies and on television,
God's witness protection program is not a matter
of hiding people away and giving them fake identities.
Rather, God's witness protection program
puts them on the streets and in the public square,
prodding them to proclaim
their identities as disciples of and witnesses to Jesus,
giving them confidence to walk along
what the Letter to the Hebrews calls
"the new and living way"
that Jesus has opened up for us.
It is not a promise that they will not suffer,
but rather that the meaning of their suffering
has already been transformed
in the resurrection and ascension of Jesus.

And this work of the Spirit
goes on in our day as well.

Last week saw the passing
of Father Daniel Berrigan,
the controversial Jesuit priest
who during his 94 years
was a consistent apostle of Christ's peace,
protesting war and the arms race,
speaking out for the rights of the defenseless,
from children in the womb to people with AIDS.
When threatened, he was not intimidated
but doubled down on his life of witness.

Whether in the pulpit,
on the streets,
or in a jail cell,
he was a constantly irritating presence
to people of all sorts of political perspectives—
not unlike Jesus,
in whose ministry of witness he shared.
Dan Berrigan walked the new and living way of Jesus,
knowing that through baptism
he had already died
and was risen with Christ.
He believed that through the Spirit,
God's promise from on high,
he was in God's witness protection program,
and that nothing could separate him
from the love of God in Christ Jesus our Lord.

As for the apostles,
as for Dan Berrigan,
so too for us.
In ascending to his Father,
Christ has promised us his Spirit,
who makes us witnesses,

giving us eyes to see the signs and wonders
that God works in our midst,
and the courage to give testimony,
to bear witness to what we have seen.
We too, through our baptism
and the Spirit's gift in confirmation,
are in God's witness protection program,
not hiding away from the intimidating task
of proclaiming Jesus crucified and risen,
not disguising our identity as Christians—
embarrassed by our belief
or fearful of giving offense—
but being willing to speak
of the transformative presence in our lives
of Jesus Christ through the Spirit,
not in order to impose our beliefs on others,
but so that those whom we meet
may themselves be witnesses and bear witness
to the reality of God's presence in the world.

26. Security Strategy

CHRISTMAS EVE

DECEMBER 24, 2017

158 *Sometimes I worry that Christmas can become an occasion for
sentimental reflection on baby Jesus and ignore the great mystery of the incarnation of God. But this year I decided to go all
in on baby Jesus. The US National Security Strategy had been
released on December 18, and I was struck by how much its rhetoric mirrored the imperial Roman rhetoric that Luke's nativity
story so cleverly subverts. Several people told me how much they
appreciated the sermon, though the parish's pastor received some
complaints that it was too negative for a celebratory family event
like Christmas. Apparently, some people think that Christmas is
not the occasion to preach on politics. I, on the other hand, can
think of no better occasion.*

READINGS: Isaiah 9:1–6; Titus 2:11–14; Luke 2:1–14

The Christmas story begins with an empire.
It begins with Caesar Augustus—
which is not a name, but a quasi-religious title
that was taken by Octavian,
the dictator who defeated two former allies
to become the sole ruler of Rome's empire
while maintaining a veneer of the old democracy.
It begins with an empire that secures peace—

the famed *Pax Romana*—
through the conquest and control of peoples.
It begins with that empire's power over "all the world,"
exercised by bureaucratic functionaries
like Quirinius, the governor of Syria,
and manifested in the tax census,
carried out to catalogue and extract
the wealth latent in the empire's conquered lands.

The outward contours of empire
have changed since the ancient world,
but the reality should be familiar to us all.
It is the aspiration to world dominance
through bluff and bluster
and sheer raw power.
We see it today in the superpowers
that jockey with each other
for military and economic hegemony.
We see it in corporations that seek to play the tune
to which the governments of the world dance.
We see it in our own nation's recently released
National Security Strategy, which assures us that
"America's values and influence,
underwritten by American power,
make the world more free, secure, and prosperous."
In fact, from the time of Octavian-called-Augustus
to that of Vladimir Putin, Xi Jinping,
and Donald Trump,
the promise of peace through dominance
has so pervaded our world,
that many have come to assume
that empire simply is the human story.
The long history of imperial power
is a tale, perhaps regrettable but nevertheless inevitable,

with which we must make our peace
if we wish to be free, secure, and prosperous.

But on this night the story of empire
is interrupted by a child.
In the middle of the tale of Octavian's power
the voice of God sounds forth
in the cries of a newborn child.
In a world ruled by wealth and power
an angel appears to poor shepherds
with good news of great joy.
In a land conquered and subjugated
by the armies of Caesar Augustus
an army of angels sings out,
"Glory to God in the highest
and on earth peace."

Just as a child might interrupt
a boring story told by adults
about the latest political scandal
or a long-term workplace rivalry
or a long-held family grudge
with his or her own fantastic tale
of dragons and magic and adventure,
so too the Christ child comes to interrupt
the tedious-yet-deadly story of worldly power
with a fantastic tale of glory and peace and joy.
Only this tale is no fantasy;
it is the very truth of God.
It is the irruption into the story of empire
of the truth that can lift the yoke of oppression
and smash the rod of the taskmaster,
the truth that consumes
every boot that tramped in battle

and every cloak rolled in blood.
In the cry of the Christ child
we hear the voice of every person
crushed beneath the yoke of power,
but we hear also the cry of the one called
"Wonder-Counselor, God-Hero,
Father-Forever, Prince of Peace."
We hear the cry of one whose dominion
is vast and forever peaceful.

And yet, the story of empire goes on.
Burdens are still laid
on the shoulders of the poor
and boots still tramp in battle.
The coming of Christ
has not brought that story to an end.
But even as the story of empire
continues its predictable narrative arc,
the voice of God in the cry of the Christ child,
in the proclamation of the angel,
in the song of the heavenly army,
interrupts that story
and begins to tell a new tale
in which we who are followers of Jesus
all play a part.

For the saving grace of God
has appeared among us in the person of Jesus
in his humble birth,
in his faithful ministry,
in his willingness to die for the truth,
in his defeat of death and rising to new life.
This grace has appeared, not rescuing us out of this world,
but "training us to reject godless ways and worldly desires

and to live temperately, justly, and devoutly in this age."
In Jesus, the interruptive grace of God
creates a new people who live a new story
as they await the final coming of Jesus,
when the story of empire will end,
and the world will know
the freedom of God's servants,
the security of God's love,
and the prosperity of God's generosity.

162   But until that day, we wait in hope,
and tell with our lives the new story
begun by Christ in the days of Caesar Augustus,
when Quirinius was governor of Syria
and Mary and Joseph made the long journey
to the city of David.
Through God's grace,
that story continues to be written in us,
when we remember those who suffer
and make their sorrows our own,
when we speak out to defend the defenseless
and to hold those in power accountable,
when we gather week by week
to tell the story of Jesus
and eat and drink his body and blood—
he who was peace in the midst of conflict,
who was hope in the midst of despair,
who was light in the midst of darkness,
who was undying life in the midst of death.
Glory to God in the highest,
and on earth peace, hope, light, and life
to those on whom God's favor rests.

27. Hope for Everything

Though many Catholic parishes tend to celebrate baptisms outside **163**
of the context of Mass, the parish where I served for the first twelve
years of my diaconate regularly celebrated baptisms at Sunday
Mass. This provided an opportunity to preach on a Sunday about
the meaning of baptism within the context of the sacramental
celebration itself. This particular Sunday was also the feast of
Christ's baptism, which (at least in some reckonings) rounds out
the Christmas season. Plus, the child being baptized, Xiomara
Kahrl, is the daughter of close friends, and I knew something of
their hopes and fears as new parents. Add to that the fact that
there was a snowstorm that prevented the musicians from mak-
ing it to Mass, forcing us to draft volunteer musicians (one of
Xiomara's godparents played piano), and you had a truly unique
set of circumstances in which to preach.

READINGS: Isaiah 40:1–5, 9–11; Titus 2:11–14; 3:4–7;
Luke 3:15–16, 21–22

Today's celebration
of the baptism of Jesus as a young man,
just as much as last week's celebration
of the visit of the magi to the baby Jesus,

is the celebration of an "epiphany,"
a "manifestation,"
an event that shows forth and reveals
the identity of Jesus as God's anointed,
the beloved Son with whom God is well-pleased.
Indeed, the baptism of Jesus is a manifestation
not only of the identity of Jesus as God's beloved
but also of the mystery of the Trinity:
Jesus the eternal Son, born now in time,
upon whom the Father sends the Holy Spirit
as he begins his time of public ministry.
The infinite, timeless dance of love that is God
shows itself in this particular historical moment,
and from this moment flows forth all that would follow:
Jesus's proclamation of God's reign,
the saving sacrifice of his passion and death,
the new dawn of his life-giving resurrection
and ascension.

In our own baptisms,
we become sharers in this epiphany.
The sacrament of baptism is an epiphany of grace;
it shows the reality of God's love
in a way that makes that love present
in this historical moment,
making us a new creation in Christ.
We become by grace what Jesus is by nature;
to everyone who rises
from the waters of baptism God says,
"This is my beloved son,"
"This is my beloved daughter."
Through baptism we share in the identity of Jesus

and become a part of that infinite,
timeless love that is God.

But what does this really mean?
What does it actually look like
to become by grace what Jesus is by nature,
to live as a son or daughter of God?
I would suggest that to be baptized into Christ
is to be invited to live out the drama of our lives
against the backdrop of an infinite horizon.
We humans can be tempted to constrain our lives
within the comfortable confines of the knowable,
to find meaning in what we at least think
we have in our control:
a career or a family,
an ethnic identity or a political ideology,
accumulated honors or achievements.
But to be baptized into Christ is to be called
beyond a life that we can control
into the wild adventure of the reign of God,
into the dizzying world-turned-upside-down
that bursts into our ordinary lives through faith in Jesus.
To be baptized into Christ is
to live within the mystery of God,
the infinite, timeless dance of love
that is the source of all life.

To put it another way,
we who have been baptized into Christ have become,
as Saint Paul puts it in our second reading,
"heirs in hope to eternal life."
If we Christians fail as Christians,

it is in hoping for too little.
We might think of the baptism of Jesus
not just as the epiphany of his divine identity
but as the epiphany of hope,
for through it we are invited to an infinite hope,
a hope for nothing less than everything.
As Saint Paul wrote to the Christians of Corinth,
"everything belongs to you . . . the world or life or death,
or the present or the future: all belong to you,
and you to Christ, and Christ to God"

(1 Corinthians 3:21–23).
This hope for everything
is planted in the hearts of all who surrender
the controllable hopes that they have for lesser things.
It is not a hope only for the strong or the wise,
for the rich or the powerful,
but for each and every life newborn in Christ,
no matter how young or how old,
how famous or how obscure,
how blessed with joys or how afflicted with sorrow.
Each is a life of infinite value,
the life of a son or daughter of God,
a life that counts in the eyes of God.

Today we will baptize Xiomara
into that hope for eternal life.
To her and to all of us who have been baptized
God says: Hope for everything.
Hope for the reign of God to be made real in you
and live a life that risks radical love;
hope to know the saving passion of Jesus in your own life
and grow in compassion for all who suffer;
hope to know the new creation

that triumphs in Christ's resurrection
and live fearlessly in the face
of opposition and misunderstanding;
hope that you may one day join your voice
to the hymn of all creation
and praise without ceasing the eternal love
in which we live and move and have our being.
For everything is yours,
and you are Christ's,
and Christ is God's.

28. Church Fires

EASTER SUNDAY

APRIL 21, 2019

168 *When the cathedral of Notre Dame burned on the Monday of Holy Week, I was firmly resolved that I was not going to mention it in my Easter homily. The symbolism of hope rising from ashes was just a bit too on the nose, and anything I might say would be at best a penetrating glimpse of the obvious. But sometimes the preacher needs to embrace the obvious, at least as an opening move. In this homily, thinking about the accidental fire at Notre Dame in light of the recent plague of deliberately set fires at African American churches became a way of thinking about how Jesus is risen not simply from the dead, but from the murdered, having been violently put to death by blind and sinful human beings. When on Easter Sunday morning nearly 150 people were killed in church bombings in Sri Lanka, I did a minor edit of the homily. Unfortunately, addressing this new act of violence fit seamlessly into what I had already planned to say.*

READINGS: Acts 10:34a, 37–43; Colossians 3:1–4; John 20:1–9

Given the timing and the weight of accumulated history, it was inevitable that people would go looking

for symbolic significance
in the fire that came close to destroying
Paris's cathedral of Notre Dame this past week.
Some suggested that it was a metaphor
for the crisis of European Christianity,
beset by decades of declining
membership and church attendance.
Others, mindful of Holy Week, saw it as a symbol
of the destruction of the temple of Christ's body—
and drew hope that Our Lady's cathedral,
like Christ himself,
would one day rise again in glory.

But maybe the lesson of the fire at Notre Dame
is not some deeply hidden message or metaphor,
but something pretty obvious:
The things we human beings construct—
no matter how beautiful or culturally significant—
catch on fire and burn.
They also rot and decay;
they get swept away in floods
and brought down by earthquakes.
And in this way they are like us, their makers.
The message of last Monday's fire
is the message of Ash Wednesday
with which we began this Lent:
Remember that you are dust,
and to dust you shall return.
Eight hundred and fifty years is a long time,
but it is not eternity;
and even if, as seems likely, Notre Dame is restored
and continues for a time as a place of Christian worship,

we know that one day this too will come to an end,
shall return to dust like everything we humans create,
as we ourselves shall as well.

Pretty somber news for an Easter morning.
But in the face of this somber news
we Christians proclaim the good news
of Jesus's resurrection.
Even as what is beautiful and noble falls to ruin,
Christ's resurrection brings us glad tidings:
We are indeed dust,
but we are dust bound for glory,
for our life is hidden with Christ in God,
and Christ is truly risen.
All that is good,
all that has value,
is treasured eternally
in the heart of the risen Jesus.

But because there has never been a silver lining
for which I could not find a dark cloud to wrap around,
I am afraid that I have news this Easter morning
even more somber than the inevitable mortality
that shadows our lives.
There is something more deeply wrong with the world
than the finite time span of every creature.
This something is what we call "sin,"
and we can see it at work in the death of Jesus.
For Jesus doesn't just die
because his human life span runs out;
rather, he is killed.
As Peter reminds the assembled crowd in Jerusalem,
"they put him to death by hanging him on a tree."

He is killed
because something far darker than death
has invaded human life.
He is killed because we have a rage within us,
a cruelty that makes us heedless of each other
and willing to cut short
the finite and fragile miracle of human life.

In a sense, the real event of recent days
that captures the full disaster of the human condition
is not the accidental fire
that nearly destroyed Notre Dame,
but the deliberate burning
of three historically Black churches in Louisiana—
and now I suppose we must add
the churches bombed and the scores of people killed
this morning in Sri Lanka.
These were, of course, far more humble structures
than the gothic glory that is Notre Dame,
but they were temples no less holy,
where worship was offered to the living God.
And while the fire at Notre Dame
speaks to us of the world's fragility and finitude,
the burning churches of Louisiana,
the bombed churches of Sri Lanka,
speak to us of sin.
They speak to us of those deeds
that grow from fear of what is different,
from a distorted sense of superiority,
from a twisted love of self,
even to the point of contempt for God and neighbor.
They speak to us of something that we can see
in our own selves,

in our own petty deeds
of fear and pride and self-involvement.

But even this somber news of sin
must yield to Easter joy.
As Peter tells the crowd gathered in Jerusalem,
"everyone who believes in him
will receive forgiveness of sins through his name."
The good news of the resurrection
is not simply that we
have been made sharers in eternal life,
but that the wounds of sin
can be healed through faith.
Our world can be different.
You and I can be different.

John's Gospel tells us that Mary Magdalene
came to Jesus's tomb "while it was still dark."
We too come to this Easter morning while it is still dark,
for the shadow of mortality and the wounds of sin
still darken our world
and make it hard for us to see the tomb standing empty.
But if we lift our eyes to the horizon,
if we heed Paul's call to "seek what is above,"
even in the darkness of death and sin
we can see the light of the resurrection
breaking in upon us,
illuminating our world
with the Spirit's gifts of faith, hope, and love.

It is still dark,
but the light of Christ's risen glory
is already dawning.

It is dawning in the people of Paris,
who, kneeling as they lift their eyes
to their beloved cathedral engulfed in flames,
sing *Je vous salue, Marie*, Hail Mary,
a song of hope in the face of tragedy.
It is dawning in the Rev. Harry Richard
of Greater Union Baptist Church
in Opelousas, Louisiana,
who says, "We've been through the fire . . .
We are heading for a resurrection."
It is dawning in you and me,
fragile and finite and, yes, sinful,
but called by God to be witnesses of Easter joy,
called by God, while it is still dark,
to reflect the light of Christ's resurrected glory.
Christ is truly risen, alleluia.

PART 5

Corona Time

There will undoubtedly be, in addition to works of history, sociology, and epidemiology, many volumes of theology written about the coronavirus pandemic. I have no plans to contribute to that body of literature. But there is a sense in which, as a preacher, you do not get to pick your topics; events simply present them to you, and you cannot ignore them. The pandemic was clearly such an unignorable event. So I offer here theological pandemic artifacts, some relics of reflections in the early days of that season I have come to think of as Corona Time.

Of course, a pandemic is unlike the events in a news cycle, which pop up and then—whether they should be or not— are quickly eclipsed by new events. The pandemic stayed and stayed, which presented a distinct homiletical challenge. It felt false to ignore it, but it was also potentially wearying to both the preacher and the listeners to keep harping on it. Of course there was much we did not know as the pandemic began, so there were new developments to talk about. But what really kept me from repeating myself over and over was the inexhaustible capacity of the Christian story to shed light on the primal hopes and fears that the pandemic unveiled.

Unlike the other homilies collected in this book, these homilies were not given in a church, but from my dining room table. As the pandemic had begun to spread, I prepared a homily, intended to be delivered in church, that addressed it, but public worship in Maryland was suspended the night before I was to give it. At my wife's suggestion, I streamed it over social media that Sunday morning instead. It got a positive reception, so my wife again suggested (insisted, really) that I prepare a homily for the following week, and I continued to do that for the fourteen weeks during which people in Baltimore could not go to church. It was certainly a different experience of preaching. It made me even more aware of the feedback loop by which the preacher draws information and energy from the faces and body language of his or her listeners. It also made me aware that, given how much time many of us spent during lockdown looking at electronic screens, it was a good idea to keep my homilies shorter than usual. Most of all, it made me aware of the importance of preaching the word in season and out of season, and especially during a pandemic.

29. Social Distancing

THIRD SUNDAY OF LENT

MARCH 15, 2020

At the beginning of March I left on a weeklong trip to visit family
in Tennessee and Montana. At my departure there were stories
coming out of China of a serious pandemic and a handful of cases
in the US. By the time I returned it was clear that we were teeter-
ing on the edge of a crisis and there was a palpable sense of tension
in the crowded airports I traveled through. As I prepared a homily
for the Third Sunday of Lent, in-person instruction had been
suspended at the university where I teach, and the suspension of
public worship seemed imminent. Already terms like "social dis-
tancing" and "flattening the curve" were entering our vocabulary,
and already it was becoming apparent that the pandemic would
hit some groups harder than others. The evening before I was to
give this homily, the next day's in-person Masses were cancelled,
so I livestreamed it from my dining room table.

READINGS: Exodus 17:3–7; Romans 5:1–2, 5–8; John 4:5–42

Among the many new things that the coronavirus
has brought into our lives
is the phrase "social distancing."
This is the term for one of the key prescriptions
for slowing the spread of the coronavirus

to the point where cases of Covid-19
do not overwhelm our medical facilities.
The idea is that you literally "keep your distance"
from other people to reduce the chance
of being infected or infecting others.

In today's Gospel, which tells of Jesus's encounter
with the Samaritan woman at the well,
we hear of a different kind of social distancing.
The woman is surprised

to have Jesus ask her for a drink
because, we are told,
"Jews use nothing in common with Samaritans."
Jews and Samaritans viewed each other as heretics
who practiced deviant forms of the religion of Israel.
But more than that, Jews considered Samaritans
to be in a sense "unclean,"
sources of a kind of religious contagion.
For the Jews, social contact with a Samaritan
was a risk to one's religious purity.
This is why the Samaritan woman is so shocked
to have Jesus ask her for water;
it is as if you asked to drink from the water bottle
of someone with a deadly disease.
This sort of social distancing sees the other
at best as one beyond my sphere of moral concern
and at worst as a threat to be contained or eliminated.
It is a phenomenon that is still with us today,
manifest in divisions of race and economic class,
of nations and generations.
We see it when people act as if
the pain and struggle of those who are different
must be kept at a distance
lest they infect us.

What do these two kinds of social distancing
have to do with each other?
The first sort is a necessary and life-saving measure
to slow the progress of this disease.
But the second sort of social distancing,
the kind that separated Jews and Samaritans,
the kind that separates races and classes in our own day,
rather than being a life-saving measure
is a death-dealing way of life.
It is death-dealing to those we keep at a distance
because it seeks to make us immune to their struggles
and deaf to their cries of suffering.
It is death-dealing to us as well,
because it requires us to harden our hearts,
to deny any natural compassion for
and solidarity with our fellow human beings.
It makes us less human,
less fully alive with the love that is God.

Jesus breaks through
this death-dealing social distancing
by the simple act of asking
the Samaritan woman for a drink of water.
Jesus bridges the social distance
between Jew and Samaritan,
breaking down the dividing wall
that separated them,
so that he can offer her the water of eternal life.
He does this not only for the Samaritan woman
but for all of us who were far from God through sin,
our hearts hardened to both God and neighbor.
Paul writes in today's second reading,
"While we were still sinners Christ died for us."
In Jesus Christ, God has opened his heart to us

and crossed the distance separating us,
and he calls us to do the same.

So we can distinguish between
the social distancing that we must undertake
in these extraordinary circumstances
and the social distancing that we must overcome
by throwing caution to the wind
and stepping across the dividing lines
of race and class and age and nationality.

Lent is a time to examine our consciences
and return to the Lord;
this public health crisis also calls for us
to examine our consciences.
I may be confident that I am healthy enough
to carry on my life as usual
and run the risk of getting sick with Covid-19,
but do I spare a thought for the elderly
or the physically frail person
with whom I come in contact
and whom I might infect?
I may feel a sense of relief
at the closing of my children's school
as a measure to protect them from infection,
but do I spare a thought for
the single working parent who will be left
without childcare if the schools close?
I may not worry about my ability
to receive excellent medical care
should I fall ill,
but do I spare a thought for the uninsured
or for those in medically underserved areas?
The death-dealing social distancing

that runs throughout our society
makes it easy to think only of ourselves
and to make ourselves blind and deaf
to those who are most vulnerable.

Our Catholic tradition calls us to care
not only for our individual well-being
but for the common good of all people.
Now is the acceptable time to embrace that tradition.
It is not only prudent that we adopt practices
of physical social distancing in order to slow
the spread of a potentially deadly disease,
but it is something that love demands.
And it is imperative that we
who are followers of Jesus
reject the social distancing that blinds us
to the needs of those most vulnerable.
Moses struck the rock in the desert
with his wooden staff
and life-giving water flowed forth.
In this season of Lent,
in this time of crisis,
may the wood of the cross
strike our stony hearts
so that the life-giving water of God's love
may flow forth from us
to quench the thirst
of those most in need.
And may God have mercy on us all.

30. Inhabiting Suffering

GOOD FRIDAY

APRIL 10, 2020

A crisis can bring out the best in people. It can also bring out the worst. It can bring out the worst in part because one person's suffering can seem to be pitted against other people's suffering. As the first weeks of the pandemic shutdown passed, I read more and more pieces in various media outlets about how some particular group's suffering was either being overlooked or overblown. It was (and is) tempting to say that our culture runs a kind of victimization sweepstakes, in which the one who can claim the worst victimhood wins. Of course, this sort of cultural critique can also be put in service of an ideological heartlessness that tells victims that they just need to "get over it" (whatever "it" is) and move on. Good Friday, however, presents us with an alternative to either of these: genuine solidarity that sees that all suffering, while variously inflected and highly particular, is still met with the one love that Christ displays on the cross.

READINGS: Isaiah 52:13–53:12; Hebrews 4:14–16; 5:7–9; John 18:1–19:42

Perhaps it is a sign of our fallen state
that we seem to treat suffering
as a zero-sum game.
We act as if the validation of one kind of suffering

somehow requires the negation
of other sorts of suffering.
This has particularly struck me
during these days of Corona Time.
A single person, suffering from isolation,
is told by those struggling to homeschool their children
that they don't know how easy they have it.
Those who speak of the tedium of staying at home
are rebuked by others in the name
of those essential workers
who must put their health at risk by leaving home
to provide for our food or medical care.
The pain of priests who cannot minister
the sacraments to their people
is pitted against the pain
of those deprived of the sacraments.
It is almost as if there is not enough
suffering to go around,
as if the recognition of one person's suffering
could somehow deprive another person
of their right to suffer.
It sounds foolish, of course, if you put it that way.
But nonetheless we do persist in feeling
that our particular form of suffering
might be invalidated if we recognize
someone suffering from different circumstances.
We treat suffering as if it were a measurable commodity
and not a mystery.

In some ways this is a failure of imagination on our part.
If I am suffering
from prolonged confinement with my family,
I can't imagine how someone could suffer
from living alone;

I suspect they must simply be complaining.
If I am putting my health at risk
to provide essential services,
I cannot imagine how not leaving the house
for days on end
could count as real deprivation.
If I am hungering to receive Christ in the sacraments,
I can't imagine that my priest
is livestreaming his private Masses
for any reason other than to taunt me.

And this failure of imagination is understandable
because, while suffering sometimes has material causes
and unmistakable outward manifestations,
at its heart it is something hidden and inward;
it is a spiritual affliction,
whatever its outward cause or sign.
It may be true, as a philosopher once said,
that the human body
is the best picture of the human soul,
but the depths of the soul's suffering
are not unfailingly depicted on the surface.
It seems still to be the case that we often fail
to grasp fully, or grasp at all, the suffering of others;
we fail in our knowing of how it is
in their particular situation.

Today, the Letter to the Hebrews reminds us
that in Jesus, "we do not have a high priest
who is unable to sympathize with our weaknesses,
but one who has similarly been tested in every way,
yet without sin."
In Jesus, God knows how it is
to be in our particular situation.
We believe that on the cross

Jesus took on the whole of the world's suffering,
not in order to satisfy in God a divine lust for vengeance,
but so that our suffering might be known from within
by the God who loves us and desires our good.
The cross is the event of divine compassion;
God suffers in the flesh in order to inhabit our suffering
so that we may "confidently approach the throne of grace
to receive mercy and to find grace for timely help."

Jesus knows your suffering, and knows it is real.
Jesus, the one without sin,
does not see your suffering as in competition with his;
indeed, your suffering is his suffering.
And he calls us who have been known by him
to see the suffering of others as he sees it,
to press beyond the limitations of our imaginations
and inhabit their suffering
as he has inhabited ours.
He calls us to listen for their suffering
and to hear it without needing to judge it
or to rank it against other suffering.
He calls us to know as he knows
that the forms of suffering
are as varied as those who suffer,
but that the remedy for our suffering
is the one love of God.
He calls us on this Friday we call good
to a deeper compassion
rooted in the compassion of the cross.
During the days and weeks ahead,
let us pray to grow in compassion.
And may God have mercy on us all.

31. On Not Returning to Normal

EASTER SUNDAY

APRIL 12, 2020

186   *One of the effects of the pandemic was a ravenous hunger for things to "return to normal" as quickly as possible, and political cunning knew how to exploit that hunger. Though only a few weeks into the shutdown, it was already apparent that this was not a fleeting phenomenon and that realistic patience, not fantasy, was the only path forward. But the suggestion was made at the highest levels of state that Easter might be our target for when "normal" could resume, which was not only unrealistic and dishonest, but fundamentally misunderstood the meaning of Easter. Christian hope is never for a mere return to normal, a restoration of an ordinary life that has been disrupted; it is hope for a transformation leading to consummation. The stories of Easter suggest both that the realization of resurrection takes time and that things never go back to "normal."*

READINGS: Acts 10:34a, 37–43; 1 Corinthians 5:6b–8;
John 20:1–9

Yesterday brought the sobering news
that the United States had surpassed
every other nation in the world
in the number of deaths
from Covid-19.

Even taking into account
the large size of our population,
the number of deaths
in hot spots like New York has been staggering.
And for someone who has lost a loved one
it doesn't really matter much
what the per capita death rates are;
it is that one death that devastates.
But even as we continue
the seemingly endless journey to peak mortality,
people have begun discussing what it will mean
to "reopen" the country:
to restart our economy,
for people to return to work,
for students to return to school,
for churches and other places of public gathering
to resume ordinary activities.
But one thing is clear:
there will be no sudden return
to so-called normal life.
It may be months still
before public Masses can be celebrated,
before children can go to school,
before we can dine in restaurants.

The idea was floated a few weeks ago
that Easter would be a nice time
for life to return to normal.
The symbolism, it might seem,
would be lovely.
But apart from the obvious error involved
in calculating the progress of the pandemic,
and differing opinions on how long
before social distancing measures

can begin to ease up,
I think the idea of Easter as a moment
when everything returns to normal
is a theologically dubious one,
and this for two reasons.

First, it is a mistake to think of Easter
as a moment, as an instant.
Of course, there is a moment
when he who was dead rises from the tomb,

but Easter is not simply
about Jesus's return to life.
Or, rather, it *is* about that,
because if it is not about that
it is not about anything.
But it is not *only* about that.
Easter is the ongoing activity of resurrection
brought about in us by Jesus through the Spirit.
In today's Gospel,
Mary Magdalene, Peter, and John
all see the empty tomb
but, we are told,
"they did not yet understand the Scripture
that he had to rise from the dead."
The reality of resurrection
that Jesus lived
was not yet fully real in them.
It seems that resurrection takes time,
and because it takes time
it involves patience,
and patience is our suffering time's passage.
The raising of Jesus from the dead
is the decisive moment:

A corner is turned,
a new reality does begin,
a new world is opened up,
but all this begins as a tiny seed
planted in the earth of humanity,
and we are still living
through the time of its growth.
Resurrection unfolds slowly
and in often hidden ways;
the new life rises in us
not on our timetable
but on God's.

Second, it is a mistake to think of Easter
as a return to normal.
As Paul tells us, we do not celebrate this feast
"with the old yeast, the yeast of malice and wickedness,
but with the unleavened bread of sincerity and truth."
Jesus is not simply resuscitated,
but transformed,
the reign of God is fulfilled in him.
As they come to share in this transformation,
the lives of Jesus's friends
do not return to normal.
Peter did not return to his nets;
Matthew did not return to his tax collecting.
As the reality of resurrection grows,
the world should become for us
stranger and stranger
until the life we live
is taken up completely
into the risen life of Christ.
As resurrection grows within us,

moments of unexpected grace
should become the new normal,
acts of extraordinary charity
should become the ordinary stuff of living,
lives lived against death and for God
should become our daily task.

If Christians truly are an Easter people,
then we who bear the name Christian
can perhaps bear witness to the watching world
about what it truly means to have hope for new life.
In the days and weeks and months ahead
we can let our resurrection faith
inform our daily living.
We can show what it means
not to look for quick fixes
but rather to willingly suffer time's passage.
We can show what it means
not to hope simply
for a restoration of the status quo,
but to think of how our world
might go forward in ways
that are more just
and more compassionate.
Whatever lies on the other side of Corona Time
is not, to be sure, the reign of God.
But perhaps it can be a world
that is just a little kinder, just a little fairer,
just a little more aligned with the truth
that Christ is risen and death is defeated.
May Christ make this new life true in us
and may God have mercy on us all.

32. A New Nearness

After a couple of months of shutdown, all novelty had worn off, and even the frisson of anxiety that had enlivened the early days of the pandemic had begun to be replaced by tedium. Perhaps most of all it was apparent to even the more introverted among us how much we humans need embodied interactions. Particularly in a strongly sacramental tradition like Catholicism, the inability to gather to celebrate the liturgy was jarring and disorienting. The physical separation we felt from family, friends, and parish community became an occasion to reflect on the mystery of the ascension, and how the absence of Jesus's physical body becomes for his disciples the occasion for an even closer unity with him and with each other through the Spirit.

READINGS: Acts 1:1–11; Ephesians 1:17–23;
Matthew 28:16–20

For most of us, the coronavirus pandemic
has been a time of distance and separation,
a time of absence from the people and things we love.
There is, of course, the literal physical distance
that we must take from people—
no closer than six feet, faces veiled by masks.

I hear the French are even thinking of abandoning
greeting one another with a kiss on each cheek.
Then there is the separation we feel
from friends and family,
an absence that technology seems unable
to really compensate for.
Nothing makes you appreciate the irreplaceability
of another person's bodily presence
like an extended Zoom visit.
There is also a strange distance

that has affected our sense of time;
early March seems years, not weeks, ago.
We are above all distant from what we might think of
as our "normal," prepandemic, selves,
so distant that we are beginning to think
that we may never recover those selves.

It might be tempting to think of the Ascension
as a feast of distance and separation and absence—
the going of Jesus to a distant place, far away from us,
his departure marking a vast distance
between us and those days
of his resurrected presence with his disciples,
a distance we try to bridge by sending up prayers,
in something like the religious equivalent of Zoom.
The joy of Easter for Jesus's friends
was having him bodily back among them,
and the ascension might seem to undo this.
And indeed, the depiction of the ascension
in the book of Acts
is something of a farewell scene:
the risen Jesus taking leave of his friends,
after which they stand around looking up at the sky,

perhaps in wonder
or perhaps with longing
to have back again the bodily presence of the risen one.

But the scene of Jesus's ascension in the book of Acts
is balanced by his final words to his disciples
in the Gospel of Matthew:
"Behold, I am with you always, until the end of the age."
The passing into heavenly glory of Jesus's risen body
does not seem to deprive his friends of his presence.
Indeed, through the gift to them of his Holy Spirit,
Jesus is somehow *more* present, *more* with them,
than he was even in his resurrected body.
I think often of Pope Benedict's description
of the ascension as "the beginning of a new nearness."
The entry of the risen Jesus into heavenly glory
does not involve him leaving here and going there,
but somehow brings here into there,
draws earth into heaven,
and in turn makes heaven present on earth
through the power of his Spirit,
who forms his followers into his body
and fills them like a temple built of living stones.
The ascension does not deprive us
of Christ's bodily presence;
rather, we become that bodily presence.
As Paul writes to the Ephesians,
God the Father "put all things beneath his feet
and gave him as head over all things to the church,
which is his body,
the fullness of the one
who fills all things in every way."
Through his ascension into glory,

Christ's body now is spread abroad
throughout the world,
for, as the poet Gerard Manley Hopkins put it,
"Christ plays in ten thousand places,
Lovely in limbs, and lovely in eyes not his
To the Father through the features of men's faces."

I think one reason why the suspension of public Masses
has been such a trial for so many people
is because it is in gathering together for worship
and receiving sacramentally the gift of Christ's body
that our identity as the body of Christ
is renewed and strengthened.
The temple built of living stones
is manifested most fully
in God's people gathered at God's altar,
and people feel keenly the absence of that gathering.
But without in any way diminishing
the real pain of absence that people are experiencing
we must believe that God
would not let us suffer this trial to no purpose.
This time of absence and distance can become,
through God's Spirit,
an experience of the "new nearness"
of the ascended Christ.
We cannot stand around looking lost,
wondering where the body of Christ has gone.
Our challenge on this day of Ascension
is to let the Spirit fill us
so that we can become his witnesses
through the fire of love
that has been poured into our hearts.
Perhaps this is what God is showing us today:

Christ's body, the church,
plays now in ten thousand places,
dispersed and yet somehow one through the Spirit.

The day will come to regather,
to receive again the body of Christ,
and it will be a day of rejoicing.
But for now we wait,
suffering time's slow passage,
trusting God to provide,
knowing that because heaven
has been joined to earth
we remain joined to one another
through the bond of the Spirit,
knowing that we are the church
even when we cannot go to church.
May God grant us the gifts of patience and love,
and may God have mercy on us all.

33. "I Can't Breathe"

196   *On May 25 the coronavirus pandemic collided with the struggle for Black lives with the killing of George Floyd by an officer of the Minneapolis Police Department. The lug nuts having been loosened by weeks of confinement, the wheels came off the societal wagon as generations of rage at injustice found new expression. It was in some ways like the unrest five years earlier following the death of Freddie Gray (see homily 4), though this time people's nerves were even more frayed and there was a base layer of anxiety already laid down by the pandemic. Covid-19 patients gasped for breath, George Floyd gasped for breath, generations of Black people gasped for breath. Could we believe that the Spirit gave breath enough to save them all?*

READINGS: Acts 2:1–11; 1 Corinthians 12:3b–7, 12–13;
   John 20:19–23

"He breathed on them and said to them,
'Receive the Holy Spirit.'"
The Spirit of life, whose very name means "breath,"
is given by means of breath
from the risen Jesus to his disciples.
Given the past few months of pandemic,
when we have masked our faces and kept our distance,

my initial response to this is a sense of dis-ease
at Jesus's casual and indiscriminate breathing on people.
But, given the past week,
the reference to breath also puts me in mind
of George Floyd with a policeman's knee on his neck
for over nine minutes,
who moaned and cried, "I can't breathe,"
until he fell silent, the spirit gone out of him.

During the pandemic shutdown I have tried
to focus on the acts of generosity and creativity
that these difficult days have elicited from people.
Despite the increasing fraying of the fabric of solidarity
in the past few weeks,
I had hoped that perhaps the pandemic
could bring out the best in us,
could point us toward a better future.
But the death of George Floyd in Minneapolis,
following swiftly on the killing
of Ahmaud Arbery in Georgia
and Breonna Taylor in Kentucky,
makes such hopes seem like idle dreams,
returning us to the old nightmare
of the persistent racism that has stained our history
as Americans, as a church, and as a human race.

But what does all of this have to do with Pentecost?
And what does the word of God
have to say to us this day?
Today we are offered both a positive vision
of the new world that the Spirit is creating
and a mandate from Christ to live in such a way
as to let God's Spirit work through God's people.

The descent of the Spirit in the book of Acts
depicts the power of God
overcoming the divisions sin has created,
as people of different lands and cultures
each hear the good news of God
proclaimed to them in their own native tongues.
Paul, writing to the Corinthians,
reaffirms the power of the Spirit
to forge unity where there had been division:
"in one Spirit we were all baptized into one body,
whether Jews or Greeks, slaves or free persons,
and we were all given to drink of one Spirit."
The good news of salvation is not simply
that our sins have been forgiven
or that death has been overcome,
but it is also that God has once more
breathed his Spirit into human clay
and brought to life a new humanity,
overcoming the divisions of race and sex and class
that have structured the world in which sin has reigned.
To be saved is not to be plucked
from this disaster of a world,
but it is to live now a transformed life
in the new world made by the Spirit.

But to say that the Spirit has called forth
a new humanity into a new world
is clearly not enough.
We who claim the name Christian
live with one foot in God's new world of grace
and one foot in the old world of sin;
we are not yet fully that new humanity
that God's Spirit would make us.

I am struck by how the risen Jesus,
appearing to his disciples,
both speaks the words "Peace be with you"
and also shows them the wounds of his torture,
as if to say, "The old world of sin is passing
and I have come with forgiveness and mercy,
but don't forget the cost of following me—
don't forget the blood and pain through which
this new world must be born."
To believe truly in Christ's message
of peace and forgiveness

we must also see the wounds
of torture and oppression.

We can focus so much
on Jesus's message of mercy and love
that we forget his call to costly repentance.
He says to his followers not only,
"Whose sins you forgive are forgiven them"
but also, "whose sins you retain are retained."
To retain someone's sin is to hold them accountable.
The ministry of forgiveness
is crucial to the life of the church,
but so is the ministry of accountability,
the ministry of not glossing over sin
when it shows itself,
the ministry of calling to repentance
so that forgiveness might become possible.
The Spirit consoles,
but the Spirit also convicts and converts.

To receive the breath of the Spirit
people have to be free to breathe it in.

And it is hard to breathe it in
with someone's knee pressing on your neck.
It is a testimony to our Black brothers and sisters
that they have over the years managed to find ways
to breathe the Spirit in despite the knees on their necks.
And it is a testimony against us who are white
that we so persistently turn a blind eye
to the wounds inflicted on the body of Christ
by the violence of racism.
The too-often repeated cry, "I can't breathe,"
is a prophetic call to see the ways in which
the Spirit who consoles
is also convicting and calling us to conversion.
May the Spirit whom we receive this day
liberate us all
and lead us to a more just world,
in which all God's children
are free to breathe the Spirit in.
And may God have mercy on us all.

PART 6

Beginnings and Endings

Perhaps the most obvious instances of preaching to specific occasions are the milestones in the human life cycle: baptisms, weddings, funerals, and so on. These endings and beginnings—and each of these milestones is really both—are always particular to those who mark them, representing key plot developments in a unique life story. Many preachers, however, have a standard sermon for baptisms, weddings, funerals, and other such moments that they give on more or less every occasion (I may have once or twice done this myself). Perhaps this is because they know that their listeners will almost surely never hear them preach it again, given the ephemeral nature of the assemblies at such events.

Given how busy those who preach often are with other things, such corner cutting is understandable. But generic homilies sound generic, even upon first hearing, so it may be worth the effort to reflect anew upon God's word for such occasions. While it may be the fourth wedding you've done in a month, it is (one hopes) the only wedding the couple will have in their life. A funeral may simply be one of many items on your agenda for the day, but it is a crucial moment—a radical ending and a new beginning—for those who will hear you preach.

The homilies collected here, however, are not of that sort. These were occasions that were significant not just to my listeners, but to me as well. They came at key moments in the life of myself, my parish, my friends, or my family. These sorts of homilies also present a special challenge to prepare and preach. When one knows the significance of an occasion, and wants to speak words of commensurate significance, one can often find oneself tongue-tied. Perhaps preachers need to give themselves permission to be less than profound, to not try to gild the lily, and to let the weight of the event itself bear the burden of profundity. On the other hand, it is at least worth trying to dig a little deeper, to honor the Word of God's encounter with the particular turning point being marked, to weave that moment in the life story of a community or individual into the great story of creation, redemption, and consummation.

34. Theo, Mary, and Ruby

FIFTH SUNDAY OF EASTER

MAY 2, 2010

This homily addresses a particular moment not simply in the lives
of three individuals, but of a community. It was not a unique
moment, inasmuch as parishes and congregations are constantly
in transition. Corpus Christi Church had been and remains a
small urban parish, with total numbers waxing and waning over
the years, but never very large by comparison with other Catho-
lic parishes. At this moment, however, we had experienced some
modest growth, which all churches say they want, though when
it happens members sometimes don't act as if they want it. The
death of a longtime parishioner, the baptism of two babies, and a
parish survey provided the occasion to reflect on the joys and chal-
lenges of growth and change within a congregation. While the
specifics are particular to this one parish, the joys and challenges
are, I think, common to all churches.

READINGS: Acts 14:21–23; Revelation 21:1–5a;
John 13:31–33a, 34–35

As many of you know,
the pastoral council's survey of the parish last year
revealed that 65 percent of those responding
have been in the parish for fewer than ten years,

and 51 percent had been in the parish
for fewer than five years.
(I should note that,
having been in the parish twelve years,
this makes me one of the "old timers"—
something I'm not too happy about.)
And if you have been paying attention
to those who tend to stand in the back of the church
you might have noticed that in the past six months
we have had something of a baby boom.

And when you add to this the seven children
we welcomed to Christ's altar
at last week's first communion celebration,
one has something of a sense
of what John felt in the book of Revelation
when he heard the voice from the heavenly throne say,
"Behold, I make all things new."

He must have felt a sense of exhilaration
at the new vistas opening up before him:
the new Jerusalem descending from heaven,
the city where God will dwell with the human race,
where "there shall be no more
death or mourning, wailing or pain,
for the old order has passed away."
At the same time,
John must have felt a sense of apprehension
at the prospect of all things being made new—
the prospect of the transformation of all that is familiar
into something new and different.
How, we might ask, will we find our way
if God makes all things new,
if the old order passes away entirely?

These thoughts occur to me at this particular moment
because on Thursday we buried Ruby Strawberry—
eighty-nine years old,
a longtime and faithful parishioner
who attended the four o'clock Saturday Mass—
and because in a few minutes we will baptize
two of our newest parishioners, Theo and Mary.
Somehow, at least in my mind, these two events
keep intersecting with each other.

It is tempting at such a moment
to think of an old order of things passing away
and a new order of things beginning,
to think of the passing of the torch
from one generation to another
as part of the ceaseless cycle of birth and death.
But there is something far more mysterious
going on here.
It is not that Theo and Mary are arriving
just as Ruby is leaving.
This might be true in terms
of the natural cycles of birth and death,
but it is not true when we take into account
the mystery of God's grace.
For our faith is that Ruby hasn't really left us;
reborn in Christ, she is not part of the old order
that has passed away,
but rather is a citizen
of the new and heavenly Jerusalem
where she dwells with God.
She is not gone;
she has simply moved more deeply
into the mystery of Christ's body,

the same body of Christ into which
Theo and Mary will soon be baptized.
By our human reckoning
Ruby might belong to one generation
and Theo and Mary to another,
but in Christ's body they share
a common birth into eternal life,
and are "fellow citizens with the saints
and members of the household of God" (Ephesians 2:19).
Somehow, in the mystery of the church,

Mary and Theo will be Ruby's friends;
they will pray for her
when our book of memory is presented each November,
and I am confident that she will pray for them
in the unfathomable eternity of the church triumphant.
This is what it means to be the church:
to believe that we are united by God's grace
in Christ's body.
And this is why Christ
commands his disciples in today's Gospel
to love one another with the same love
with which he has loved them.
This is the love that can unite us
across barriers of time and distance,
and even across the barrier of death.

It is important always to keep
this love that Christ commands before our eyes
as we live our life together as a community of faith.
Given human nature, we can be tempted
either to cling to the past,
to the ways that we have always done things,

or to become so enamored of the new
that we dismiss our heritage
as merely part of the old order that has passed away.
Both temptations must be resisted
if we are to fulfill Christ's command of love.
The one who says, "Behold, I make all things new"
constantly calls us into a future that requires us to change,
to think in new ways,
to venture outside the boundaries
with which we are comfortable.
The influx of new parishioners
in the past decade
is a wonderful sign of life
but is also a challenge to those of us
who have been around a while:
a challenge to think in new ways
and to ask new questions,
to listen to new voices
and consider new possibilities.
At the same time,
we have a body of accumulated wisdom:
the wisdom of our longtime parishioners
and the wisdom of the tradition of the church,
and this too must be listened to
if we are to be faithful to who we are.

What will make all of this possible is love:
the love with which Christ loves us
and with which he commands us to love each other.
Like Mary and Theo and Ruby,
we meet on the common ground of the love of Christ,
trusting that Christ crucified and risen is in our midst,

and that God's Spirit is here to guide us.
Our treasured past,
our challenging present,
and our unknown future
are all united in the God
whom Saint Augustine called
the "beauty so ancient and so new."
So let us love one another—
old timers and newcomers,
children and adults,

progressives and traditionalists.
Let us love one another with the same love
with which Christ has loved us.
We owe it to Mary and Theo.
We owe it to Ruby Strawberry.
We owe it to ourselves.

35. Restless Hearts

My father-in-law, Clayton Sweeney, was one of eight children
in a large Irish Catholic family in Pittsburgh. Perhaps that tells
you enough to know that the feelings engendered by his death
were complex, intense, and largely repressed. Most preachers at
funerals are blessed with, at best, a superficial familiarity with
the deceased, which makes them blissfully ignorant of the various
land mines that they should try to navigate around. I was not,
in this case, so blessed. Instead I was blessed with the burden of
knowledge and a desire to speak a word both consoling and truth-
ful, acknowledging the flaws of a great man and honoring the
good done by a fallible human being. But most of all I wanted to
preach the gospel of hope and resurrection in light of a particular
life that had now reached the end of its pilgrimage. It was my
wife, Maureen, who suggested to me that her father's life was a
reflection of Augustine's words about our restless hearts.

READINGS: Isaiah 25:6a, 7–9; Revelation 21:1–5a, 6b–7;
Matthew 11:25–30

Clayton Sweeney was a busy man.
Of course, no one who raises six children
gets much downtime,

even if he has a force of nature like Sally Dimond
to do a lot of the parental heavy lifting.
But you can add to that his work
as a lawyer, a corporate executive,
a board member, an adjunct law professor—
not to mention the almost full-time job
of being a sibling to his brother and six sisters,
and an uncle to literally scores of nieces and nephews,
for whom he was always a source
of willing and generous support.

Even in his so-called retirement at Lake Chautauqua—
his own version of Yeats's Lake Isle of Innisfree,
where he sought the peace that "comes dropping slow/
Dropping from the veils of the morning
to where the cricket sings"—
even there his life was a flurry of activity:
serving on the boards of numerous nonprofits,
singing in the choir at his beloved parish
of Saint Isaac Jogues in Sherman,
hosting an endless stream of family and friends
and friends of friends in his home,
and keeping track of the exploits and misadventures
of his ten grandchildren.
All of this activity bore fruit in a long list
of noteworthy achievements
and significant contributions
to his family, his church, and his community.
Clayton was a busy man in part
because he was an extraordinarily talented man
who was often called upon
by groups and individuals for his expertise,
and because he was also

an extraordinarily generous man
he rarely said no.

But now we have come to lay this busy man to rest.

When the early Christian theologian
Saint Augustine wrote,
"You have made us for yourself, O God,
and our heart is restless until it rests in you,"
he put his finger on something
fundamental about being human:
We are made by God to live with God,
and God alone can quench
our thirst for meaning and love.
No achievement, no honor, no paycheck or bonus
can still the restless seeking of our hearts,
but only the one who says, "Come to me,
all you who labor and are burdened,
and I will give you rest."
For all his achievements and honors,
Clayton remained not just a busy man,
but a restless man.

It does not diminish Clayton's memory
to say that he was not perfect,
to say that in the restless journey of his life
he labored and was burdened,
for we know that we are saved by God's mercy,
not by our own perfection.
So, for example, it was rumored
that Clayton could be a bit stubborn
(a trait that he passed along

to at least a few of his children),
and it could be quite terrifying
to watch a Steelers game with him,
particularly if things were going badly.
But he also struggled with demons
more troubling and more difficult to face,
demons that were hardly unique to him,
but seem, in one guise or another, to afflict all of us
in our restless journey through this life.

In the almost thirty years that I knew Clayton,
it seems to me that his greatest burden,
his greatest source of unrest,
was the struggle to let those whom he loved
know just how deeply he loved them.
Again, this struggle is hardly unique to him;
all of us want so badly to let those whom we love
know how much we love them,
but often the words don't come,
or they come out wrong.
Even the best of us,
who busy ourselves with all we can do for others,
all we can give to those whom we love,
can still hold back ourselves,
perhaps afraid that the naked gift of ourselves
will not be enough to merit love in return.

When Clayton died
I posted a picture of him on Facebook
from his seventieth birthday celebration.
He was surrounded by his ten grandchildren,
all engaged in various acts of mischief and misbehavior,
and Clayton looked as happy as I have ever seen him.

It garnered a number of comments,
but one in particular stood out to me:
"What a golden picture, and a foretaste. Eternal rest."
It was a picture of a happy moment from the past,
but also, I think, a picture
of what we now hope for Clayton.
On our restless journey through this life
we are sustained by the grace-filled glimpses
we are granted
of what it must be like to rest in God.
For the seer John in the book of Revelation
it was the image of a new heaven and a new earth
in which God would dwell with humanity.
For me, it is that golden picture,
which captures the busy man in a moment of rest,
surrounded by squirming grandchildren who, like God,
loved him not for anything he had done
but for who he was,
loved him not for anything he had achieved
but simply because he was their Papa.
"Although you have hidden these things
from the wise and the learned
you have revealed them to little ones."

Clayton was a busy man,
a restless man who achieved much,
but in the end I think that he, like all of us,
wanted only this:
to love and be loved for who he was.
And he, like all of us, was burdened by the fear
that who he was would not be good enough.
But now he can lay that burden down.
Now he knows,

through the mercy of Christ,
it is enough;
it was always enough.
Now he is surrounded,
as in that golden picture,
by the love of God,
the love that will strip away from him
all that is fearful, all that is false,
and reveal him to himself as who he truly is:
Clayt, Dad, Papa, brother, uncle, friend,
beloved child of the living God.
The busy, restless man is now at rest.

It seems appropriate in this place to end with words
from another notable Catholic lawyer:
Saint Thomas More.
On the night before he was executed
he wrote to his daughter Margaret
words that I believe Clayton even now is saying to us:
"Farewell, my dear child, and pray for me,
and I shall for you,
and for all your friends,
that we may merrily meet in heaven."

Until then, Clayton, rest in peace.

36. Of Whales and Fleas

WEDDING OF TRENT POMPLUN AND SAMANTHA O'CONNOR

OCTOBER 8, 2016

Over the years I have preached at a lot of weddings. I always try **215** *to personalize my words to some degree, by discussing with the couple their reasons for choosing the particular Scripture readings that they did, as well as gaining some sense of how they met, their commonalities and differences, and so forth. But this wedding was different, being the wedding of two friends whom I had known individually even before they knew each other. I knew, for example, that it was a shared passion for the novel* Moby Dick *that had initially brought them together. I knew (as a "meet cute" involving a nineteenth-century novel might suggest) their intellectual intensity and, to be honest, quirkiness. It was a joy and an honor to preach and preside at their wedding, and I felt that they deserved nothing less than a homily on* Moby Dick.

READINGS: **Genesis 2:18–24; 1 Corinthians 12:31–13:8a; John 17:20–26**

Ishmael, the narrator of Melville's *Moby Dick*,
after commenting on the dizzying effects
of trying to write about a creature like the whale, says:
"Such, and so magnifying,
is the virtue of a large and liberal theme!

We expand to its bulk.
To produce a mighty book,
you must choose a mighty theme.
No great and enduring volume
can ever be written on the flea,
though many there be who have tried it"
(*Moby Dick*, chapter 104).
What Ishmael says of books
might also be said of marriages:
No less than a book, a marriage must have a theme,

something that gives it a direction and a meaning;
and a great and enduring marriage,
no less than a great and enduring volume,
must have a mighty theme,

Because marriage involves the most private, intimate love
of a man and a woman,
it is tempting to think that this should be its theme.
To quote the immortal Sonny Bono:

> They say we're young and we don't know,
> We won't find out until we grow.
> Well I don't know if all that's true,
> 'Cause you got me, and baby I got you.
> I got you babe.

But as important as the intimate love
of a man and a woman is
(and who am I to doubt Sonny Bono?),
I would suggest that for Christians
this is an insufficiently mighty theme
upon which to base a great and enduring marriage,
though many there be who have tried it.

In our first reading, from the book of Genesis,
marriage is given a cosmic significance:
God created human beings for companionship
and the mutual love of the man and the woman
are part of the perfection of God's creation.
When Adam says, "This one, at last,
is bone of my bones and flesh of my flesh,"
we can feel his joy, not simply in finding a companion
but in discovering a possibility
newly born within the cosmos.
That possibility is opened up

by one with whom he can enter
into a free and equal exchange of love,
in which love is given to another
and then received back, transformed, increased,
ready to be given and received
again and again, day by day,
growing and overflowing into love
for all that God has made,
reflecting God's own free love
for the world God has made.

But for Christians this cosmic dimension of marriage
is perhaps not yet a mighty enough theme.
In our reading from John's Gospel,
Jesus prays to his Father for his disciples,
that, "the love with which you loved me
may be in them and I in them."
This is a love that goes beyond human love
because it is the love with which the Father loved Christ
"before the foundation of the world."
But it is also a love that Jesus desires
to share with his disciples

so that "they may be brought to perfection as one,"
and so become for the world a sign
of the God who is love.
In the Catholic tradition,
we teach that marriage is a sacrament,
which means that it is a human reality
by which God shares his love with us.
If marriage is taken up as a form of discipleship,
if it takes as its theme
the love revealed in the cross and resurrection of Jesus,

then the joining together
of husband and wife is not simply
a part of the perfection of creation,
but it becomes a means of grace,
a way in which divine love comes to dwell in our world
to heal and to save and to bring joy.
Compared with the immensity of this theme,
this event of divine love invading our world,
the theme of "I got you babe"
seems small and flea-like,
unworthy of the great and enduring love
that we pray will pervade and sustain
the marriage of Trent and Sammy.

Trent and Sammy, I am uncharacteristically hopeful
that you will not rest content
with a small and flea-like theme for your marriage.
Face it: You have a tendency to go overboard.
Knowing as I do your tendencies to excess—
excessive books and wine,
excessive theological and literary conversations,
excessive scholarly conscientiousness,
excessive worrying over wedding preparations—

I feel confident that you will settle for nothing less
as the theme for your marriage
than that "still more excellent way"
of which Saint Paul writes
in his letter to the Corinthians:
the mighty love that "bears all things,
believes all things,
hopes all things,
endures all things."
And I feel confident that God's grace
will be there to expand your love for each other,
to fill the bulk of this great and whale-like theme,
to help you endure together
through the daily crosses of suffering you will face,
to help you rejoice together
in the daily resurrections of joy that God will give you,
until that day when the perfect comes
and the partial passes away,
that day when we will see no longer dimly,
as in a mirror,
but face to face,
knowing fully,
even as we are known,
that day of which
the joy of *this* day,
great as it is,
is but a sign,
the day of the great wedding feast of the Lamb.
May God's grace bring the two of you,
through the love you vow this day,
to that feast.

37. Current

220 *My reassignment from Corpus Christi Church, where I spent my first twelve years as a deacon, was not something I chose for myself. I could have said no, but a promise of obedience inclines one to say yes. So my departure was undertaken freely, even if not by my own initiative. This was the community that had been my family's spiritual home for two decades, where my children had received their first Eucharist, where I had preached on Sundays and presided at numerous baptisms and weddings, where I knew people and people knew me. But, as both Saint Augustine and my son the whitewater raft guide have taught me, pilgrimage through this life allows us no permanent resting places. We are sustained, however, by a companionship that time and space cannot destroy, a fellowship in broken bread that is Christ's body.*

READINGS: 1 Kings 19:16b, 19–21; Galatians 5:1, 13–18;
Luke 9:51–62

As many of you might know,
last month I spent two and a half weeks
traveling by raft with family and friends
down the Colorado River
through the Grand Canyon.

The thing about this sort of trip
is that once you set out
you are committed for the long haul;
except for a lengthy hike to the canyon rim
or a quick but costly medevac by helicopter,
there is only one way to the journey's end,
only one direction that the current flows,
only one takeout point, many days and miles ahead.

I knew this, of course,
in a theoretical way
before setting out,
but you don't really know
what you've gotten yourself into
until you've tried to set up camp in the rain,
or spent an hour pumping river water through a filter
so that there would be something to drink,
or taken a four-hour side hike
that ends up lasting seven hours,
or stood above a class-nine rapid
listening to more experienced boaters discuss
all of the places in the rapid
where you definitely *don't* want to end up.
The trip was much more arduous and challenging
than I anticipated,
the kind of vacation
where you need
another vacation afterward,
just to recover.

But the current flowed just one way;
there was no going back,
even if at times I wondered

what I had gotten myself into.
And it was a good thing that I had no choice,
that quitting was not an option
and weariness or fear could not change my course,
because along the way I saw wonders
that I could not have seen in any other way:
crystal-blue waters flowing from side canyons,
billion-year-old stone walls;
bighorn sheep climbing sheer rock faces;
the undimmed stars crowding the night sky;
the violent pounding force of the rapids;
and people of varied background, skill, and ability
working together to make the journey possible.

I say all of this not just to let you know
that I had an awesome vacation—
though it *was* awesome
(in the literal sense of the term).
Rather, at the risk of turning
a geologic marvel into a metaphor,
I can't help thinking of how such a journey
tells us something about the journey
of our life as followers of Jesus.

Jesus says in today's Gospel
that once you set out
on the journey to God's kingdom,
once you embark
on the adventure of being his disciple,
you are committed for the long haul:
"No one who sets a hand to the plow
and looks to what was left behind
is fit for the kingdom of God."

He warns his followers, repeatedly,
of the arduous and challenging nature of the journey:
"Foxes have dens and birds of the sky have nests,
but the Son of Man has nowhere to rest his head."
But it is only along the way that we discover
exactly what it is that we have gotten ourselves into:
the labor of being people of faith, hope, and love;
the perils of misunderstanding and rejection;
the thirst we feel in times of doubt and spiritual dryness;
the struggle to keep our hand on the plow
and not look back at what we have left behind.
But there is no turning back
because we are caught in the current of the Spirit
who carries us forward on the journey.
And thanks be to God for that,
for it is along this arduous way
that we discover wonders:
the beauty of God revealed
in the face of Jesus,
the glory of God shown forth
in the word and sacraments,
the love of God displayed in the lives
of those who travel with us on the journey.
This journey with Jesus
leads us into the very meaning of existence.

It is a journey we share together,
each of us bringing with us
our varied backgrounds, skills, and abilities.
It is a journey that is held in common
and yet is also unique to each of us.
We share common milestones that mark the way:
baptism, confirmation,

our weekly gathering at the Eucharist.
We each also have
our individual milestones
by which we chart our journey:
joys, sorrows,
losses, triumphs,
illnesses, friendships,
marriages, religious vows,
births, deaths.
But in the body of Christ
these individual milestones are
in some mysterious way,
through the one Spirit that we all share,
also part of our common journey.
Your joys become my joys,
your sorrows become my sorrows.

Twelve years ago,
immediately before I was ordained as a deacon
through the laying on of hands and prayer,
I knelt before Cardinal Keeler
with my hands joined in front of me.
He put his hands around mine, asking,
"Do you promise respect and obedience
to me and my successors?"
and I replied, "I do."
Then the cardinal said,
"May God who has begun the good work in you
bring it to fulfillment."
Amid all the ritual and symbolism
of the rite of ordination,
this moment has always stood out for me.
This promise of obedience was a milestone
that made concrete for me

something that had been true
since the day of my baptism:
my life belongs not to me but to the journey,
and to belong to the journey is to be truly free.
It was not simply about submitting
to ecclesiastical authority,
but about listening for the voice of Jesus
when he calls us to leave behind the things we love
and step into the current of the Spirit
so that the wonders of the journey
might be brought to fulfillment
in the freedom that comes
from answering Christ's call.

This, of course, is true for every follower of Jesus.
As Paul says, "you were called for freedom."
All of us must listen for his voice
calling us into the current of the Spirit.
The difference for me, as an ordained person,
is that the voice of Jesus—as strange as this may seem—
can sound like the voice of the archbishop of Baltimore.
And it seems that the voice of Jesus
is calling me to leave behind this community that I love
so that our common journey can continue in a new way.
This is one of those arduous,
challenging moments of the journey.
This is one of those moments when you wonder
what you have gotten yourself into.
This is one of those moments
when you must tighten your grip on the plow
and step forward in faith.

I have worshipped with you for twenty-two years
and served you as deacon for twelve,

and quite honestly it is hard for me to imagine
what it will be like not to gather with you each Sunday.
But if it truly is the current of the Spirit
that moves us forward on the journey,
if it is in answering the call of Jesus
that we find true freedom,
then we must trust that new wonders
will be revealed to us along the way.
And if it is truly the one Spirit
in whose current we are floating

then we are still journeying together,
even when it seems that we are separated.
For we all, wherever Christ calls us to be,
however scattered in time and space,
remain together members of his body: *Corpus Christi*.
This is perhaps the greatest wonder of all.

Index of Names and Subjects

Index of Scripture